Y0-BXD-350

SECRETARY'S PORTFOLIO OF INSTANT LETTERS

Anne Wayman

PRENTICE HALL
Englewood Cliffs, New Jersey 07632

Prentice-Hall International (UK) Limited, *London*
Prentice-Hall of Australia Pty. Limited, *Sydney*
Prentice-Hall of Canada, Inc., *Toronto*
Prentice-Hall Hispanoamericana, S.A. *Mexico*
Prentice-Hall of India Private Limited, *New Delhi*
Prentice-Hall of Japan, Inc., *Tokyo*
Simon & Schuster Asia Pte. Ltd., *Singapore*
Editora Prentice-Hall do Brasil, Ltda., *Rio de Janeiro*

10 9 8 7 6 5 4 3 2

Library of Congress Cataloging-in-Publication Data

Wayman, Anne.
Secretary's portfolio of instant letters / by Anne Wayman.
p. cm.
Includes index.
ISBN 0-13-798521.-5
1. Commercial correspondence—Handbooks, manuals, etc. 2. Letter writing—Handbooks, manuals, etc. I. Title.
HF5726.W28 1990
808'.066651—dc20 89-16020
CIP

ISBN 0-13-798521-5

Printed in the United States of America

Acknowledgments

A book like this wouldn't be possible without the help of many others. I'd like to thank the following:

The Biltmore Hotel; Coldwell Banker; The Coastal Post; The Crystal Palace; E & L Engineering, Fallbrook Real Estate Co.; First American Bank; Galilee Harbor Community Association, Inc.; Huntington Beach Church of Religious Science; In The Public Eye; Kaypro, Inc.; Long Beach and Sausalito Chambers of Commerce; Mariners of Richardson Bay; Mill Valley Record; Oberg and Sindicich, Attorneys at Law; Ocean Medical Services, Inc.; Peregrine Falcon Co.; Software for Sale; Profiles Magazine; Quantum Productions; UK Sails, Sausalito; University of California at Santa Barbara; Waterside Productions; Wayman of Fallbrook; Western Temporary Services, Inc.

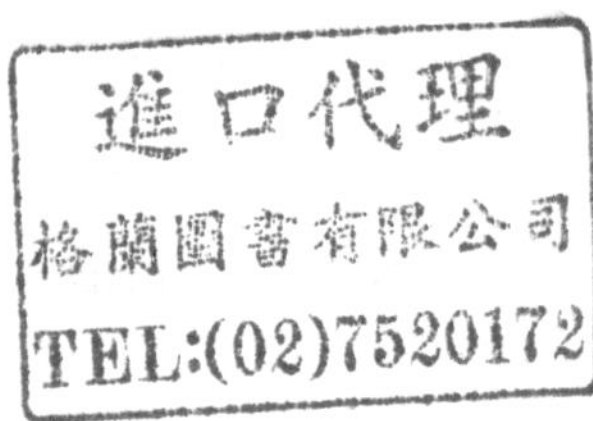

What the Secretary's Portfolio of Instant Letters Will Do For You

The *Secretary's Portfolio of Instant Letters* provides a quick, easy, and efficient method to generate all the effective correspondence your business needs without wasting your valuable time.

Secretaries know that letter writing is a critical part of their job. Yet while many letters are standard, hardly a day passes without the need to create a letter that handles a situation outside the normal office routine. So most secretaries report they keep copies of particularly effective letters, thereby creating a personal collection of correspondence for future reference.

This *Portfolio* gives you not only a collection of letters secretaries write every day but also letters that are not routine, thus saving hours of research and dozens of rough drafts.

Letters included in the *Portfolio* are drawn from large, small, and medium size businesses. The names and addresses have been changed to protect privacy, but the content has been tested to get desired results.

Special attention has been paid to unusual situations, including the letters needed for nonprofit organizations and the communications necessary for developing positive relations with the press. Everything from establishing and purging a mailing list to responding to computer-generated letters and getting results can be found in this book.

Because of the research that has gone into the over 300 letters contained in the *Portfolio*, secretaries will find they can often use the content verbatim. Yet even when that isn't possible, only minimal changes will be needed, and the result will be letters that are effective and to the point.

How to Use This Book

The *Secretary's Portfolio of Instant Letters* is organized to make the secretary's job easier. To help achieve this, the book is set up in the following way:

- The book is divided into 12 Chapters, each reflecting a particular category of letter the secretaries need. The Parts are arranged in logical order, beginning with the internal office and working out to the public.
- Each Chapter is further categorized with Sections that address specific areas of responsiblity.
- Each Chapter and Section is listed in the Table of Contents, along with the name of each letters.
- Each letter also has optional phrases that offer a change in tone and may spark your imagination.
- Recognizing it is impossible to include every letter you'll ever need, each Chapter is prefaced by specific information and tips about writing effective letters in that particular category.

Finally, Chapter 12 is a text on effective business letter writing, giving you all the information you need to write letters that will get you the results you want. Included are the following:

- Powerful writing
- Achieving a balanced writing style
- Punctuation, sentences and paragraphs
- Avoiding cliches, redundancies and boredom with word lists and examples
- A guide to non-sexist letter writing
- Mistakes in common usage
- A word about word processing
- A checklist to help you be certain each letter you write contains exactly the needed elements

The Secretary's Portfolio of Instant Letters covers almost every letter a secretary will need and contains the information needed to compose letters from scratch. By scanning either the Table of Contents or the Index, you'll find an appropriate sample letter. From there, it's a simple matter to put the exact letter you want on your letterhead.

The Secretary's Portfolio of Instant Letters will make your job easier and make you look good. It's so efficient, you'll wonder how you ever did without it.

Table of Contents

Chapter 1

LETTERS CONCERNING THE OFFICE

LETTERS ABOUT THE PHYSICAL PLANT

Lease Renewal
Notice of Lease Termination by Tenant
Notice of Lease Termination by Landlord
Requesting Plumbing Repair
Requesting Special Cleaning
Requesting Different Lighting
Asking about Facilities in New Building

LETTERS ABOUT OFFICE SUPPLIES AND EQUIPMENT

Confirming a Telephone Order for Business Cards
Confirming a Telephone Order for Stationery
Written Order for Business Cards Enclosing Camera Ready Art
Requesting an Office Supply Catalog
Requesting Credit for Office Supplies
Ordering Supplies - Table in Letter
Requesting Bids for Copier Service
Changing Standing Order for Copier Supplies
Explaining a Problem With Copier Service
Canceling Water Delivery
Asking for a Change in Coffee Service

LETTERS DEALING WITH EMPLOYMENT AND EMPLOYEES

INVITATIONS TO BUSINESS SOCIAL FUNCTIONS

LETTERS CONCERNING SUBSCRIPTIONS

TRAVEL ARRANGEMENTS

TRANSMITTAL LETTERS

As a secretary you will often be called upon to gather information and solve problems that have to do with the actual day-to-day running of the office. For example, in a relatively short time, you may find yourself writing letters to the office building's owner concerning plumbing problems, to potential suppliers requesting bids for office equipment, to employees and potential employees, and to thank someone for special services

You'll often know exactly what the situation is and what needs to be done. Sometimes, however, you may find yourself dealing with unfamiliar information. Yet in either a familiar or unfamiliar situation, your letters will not only communicate the necessary information but will also provide a written record of that communication.

This section offers sample letters addressing a variety of situations. You will find the letters useful not only because many of them can be used almost verbatim but because they will also spark your thinking about exactly what needs to be said.

SECRETARY'S TIPS ON WRITING LETTERS CONCERNING THE OFFICE

1. *Be sure you understand the purpose of the letter.* Letters concerning the office fall generally into two categories, solving problems or providing information. If you're not clear about the problem to be solved or the information to be provided, your letter will not be clear. Take the time to be sure you know exactly what results you want from the letter.
2. *Get all the information you need before composing the letter.* Many letters concerning the office will be straightforward, and you'll have all the information you need in your head or at your fingertips. Some, however, will deal with topics you have little or no understanding of. If you feel you need more information, get it before you attempt to write the letter. In

the long run, you'll save time, and your letter will do a better job of communicating.

3. *Determine the tone of the letter.* The tone of your letter will be determined both by the subject matter and by your relationship with the reader. A quick note confirming a telephone order to a supplier you work with on a regular basis will be much more informal than an official notice of termination of lease to your landlord. It's probably better to err on the side of formality, as long as you don't sound pompous.

   The "author" of the letter will determine what tone to use. In many cases, the letter may appear over your signature; in other cases it should be signed by someone who has more authority.

4. *The first paragraph should contain the most important information.* Everyone in business is inundated with thousands of printed words daily. By keeping the most important information in the first paragraph, you increase the chances that the reader will readily understand the purpose of the letter. The balance of the letter should then amplify and explain that purpose.

5. *Make it clear what response, if any, is expected from the reader.* Let the recipient of your letter know exactly what response or action is expected. If there's a deadline, spell it out; if you want a written response, say so; if you're going to follow up with a phone call, give the reader a time frame in which to expect your call. On the other hand, if the letter is for informational purposes only, make that clear also.

6. *Be concise and complete.* Find the balance between being brief and being complete. If you don't give enough information, the recipient won't be able to respond; if you give too much, your letter may not be read completely. If possible, limit your letters about office business to one page, but don't hesitate to use as many pages as you actually need.

LETTERS ABOUT THE PHYSICAL PLANT

LEASE RENEWAL

Dear Mr. Guenther:

Enclosed is our lease renewal, signed and initialed as you requested. We have kept a copy for our records.

We are pleased to continue in our present location and appreciate your cooperation.

Sincerely,

Alternative Phrases:

- We truly like our present location. We also appreciate your responsive management.

NOTICE OF LEASE TERMINATION BY TENANT

Dear Mr. Bowers:

This letter will serve as the written notice required in our lease that we intend to terminate and vacate our lease ninety (90) days from today.

We will, of course, leave the premises as we found them, and expect to receive our security deposit within ten (10) days of our returning the key to you.

If you have any questions, please call.

Sincerely,

NOTICE OF LEASE TERMINATION BY LANDLORD

Dear David:

I know you've heard the rumors that West Marine is going to expand. We completed the arrangements today and wanted to let you know that we will expect you to vacate your premises one hundred eighty (180) days from today.

Since we recognize this will disrupt your business, we are willing to waive the sixty-day notice should you arrange for new quarters during the next six months.

We'd also be delighted to give you an excellent reference if that would be helpful.

Sincerely,

Alternative Phrases:

- As you are probably aware, West Marine is planning on expanding its store. Although you are on a month-to-month tenancy with us, we are giving you a full 180-day notice to vacate as of the date of this letter.
- Because we recognize this change may cause some disruption, we are willing to reduce your requirement to give us sixty days notice to thirty days.

REQUESTING PLUMBING REPAIR

Dear Annie:

The toilet off our reception area won't stop running. We've fiddled with it with no success. Since you pay for the water in the center and are responsible for this type of repair, I know you'll want to get this fixed as soon as possible.

We're open from 8:00 A.M. to 5:00 P.M., Monday through Friday, so you can have your plumber come any time during those hours.

If you have any questions, give me a call—otherwise, we'll keep our eyes open for the plumber.

Sincerely,

Alternative Phrases:

- Even though we pay for the water, our lease agreement holds you responsible for repair. Please have your plumber fix this as soon as possible.
- If you'll have your plumber give us a call, we'll make sure someone is here.

REQUESTING SPECIAL CLEANING

Dear Joan:

On September 16, we are having an open house and would like to make arrangements for you and your crew to do a special cleaning on September 15 in preparation.

In addition to the usual dusting and vacuuming, I'd like you to pay special attention to the windows, both inside and out. We will, of course, expect to pay extra for the window cleaning.

Let me know if this is a problem. I'll give you a call next week to confirm.

Thanks so much for your help.

Sincerely,

Alternative Phrases:

- Please give me a call and let me know what the window washing will cost.
- Please give me a call next week to confirm the arrangements.

REQUESTING DIFFERENT LIGHTING

Dear Mr. Thomas:

This will confirm our telephone conversation today about changing the lighting in our store. You have agreed to replace the "cool white" fluorescents with "day glow" by the end of the month, and we have agreed to reimburse you one hundred dollars ($100.00) for the difference in purchase cost within thirty days of the completed installation.

Please be sure to give me a call before you actually make the change so that we can make arrangements to stay out of your way.

Thanks so much for your help.

Sincerely,

Alternative Phrases:

- Thanks for stopping by the store and agreeing to help us change the lighting.
- Let me know when you schedule the change so that we can plan for the interruption.
- Thank you for your help.

ASKING ABOUT FACILITIES IN NEW BUILDING

Dear Mr. Jordan:

Thank you for the brochure on your new office building. It looks good, but we have some questions:

1. Will there be assigned parking? If so, how will it be assigned?
2. Are you planning a coffee room or other common area where employees might be able to eat lunch?
3. If we take advantage of sharing secretarial services with other com-

panies in the building, how will the secretarial staff be chosen? How will we be charged?

We're looking forward to your response.

Sincerely,

Alternative Phrases:

- We enjoyed spending some time in your new office building.
- We are interested in leasing space in your building on Seventh Street.
- It appears to meet our needs.

LETTERS ABOUT OFFICE SUPPLIES AND EQUIPMENT

CONFIRMING A TELEPHONE ORDER FOR BUSINESS CARDS

Dear Mary:

This letter will confirm our telephone order for business cards.

Please use our usual art work, Eaton Ivory card stock, and Pantone Reflex Blue C ink. We would like 500 each of the following names:

Janice McKinney, Sales Representative

Michael "Mike" Wilder, Sales Representative

Bev Slade, Director of Marketing

We will expect delivery to our office in ten days and to be billed "net 30 days" as usual.

If you have any questions, please call me.

Sincerely,

CONFIRMING A TELEPHONE ORDER FOR STATIONERY

Dear Mr. Barnes:

This letter will confirm our telephone order for stationery and envelopes using the new art work, which is enclosed. Go ahead with the classic laid stock, using Bordeaux ink. We'd like 5,000 letterheads, 5,000 second sheets with no printing, 5,000 printed envelopes, and 2,500 printed window envelopes.

Enclosed is our deposit check for two hundred fifty dollars ($250). We will expect delivery in about fifteen days and will pay the balance sixty days from delivery.

Please give me a call if you have any questions or if you anticipate a delay.

Sincerely,

Alternative Phrases:

- We request that you use the classic laid stock . . .

WRITTEN ORDER FOR BUSINESS CARDS ENCLOSING CAMERA READY ART

Dear Duncan:

We did it! We finally created a business card we like with our computer and laser printer. Our camera-ready art is enclosed. Also enclosed are the typeset names and, in some cases, home phone numbers.

We'd like 500 cards for each of the enclosed names on gray classic laid stock, using the same burgundy ink as usual.

If you have any questions, please call.

Sincerely,

Alternative Phrases:

- Our graphic artist has come up with a business card design we like; enclosed is camera-ready art.
- Enclosed is the camera-ready art for our business cards.
- Beside each name is the number of cards we'd like for that individual.

REQUESTING AN OFFICE SUPPLY CATALOG

Dear Sir/Madam:

Please send us your office supply catalog as advertised in the September issue of *Today's Secretary.*

Sincerely,

Alternative Phrases:

- Enclosed is (dollar amount) for your office supply catalog as advertised . . .

REQUESTING CREDIT FOR OFFICE SUPPLIES

Dear Sir/Madam:

We would like to establish a credit line with you of one hundred and fifty dollars ($150) per month. We expect to be purchasing our copier paper from you, in addition to other office supplies.

Please feel free to check the following references:

Sears Savings Bank, Seal Beach Branch, Ms. Karen Fair, Manager, (213) 555-7878

Mr. Jonathan Miller, owner and manager of our office building, (213) 555–6868

If you need any more information, please call. Also, we'd like to know when the account is approved.

We're looking forward to doing business with you.

Sincerely,

Alternative Phrases:

- We expect to be purchasing our copier paper from your company, . . .
- We have established a credit history with the following:
- Please call me when the account is approved.
- Please send a copy of our charge number when the account is approved.

ORDERING SUPPLIES—TABLE IN LETTER

Dear Sir/Madam:

Please send us the following office supplies:

7 boxes, Bic medium point, blue ink
4 reams 20# white bond
10 boxes of Verbatim 5¼″ DSDD floppy disks

Our charge account number is 73A-34-65.

We will expect delivery by UPS.

Sincerely,

REQUESTING BIDS FOR COPIER SERVICE

Dear Sir/Madam:

We have a Xerox 714 with collator, a Kodak 2100, and four Sharp personal copiers. Some days we run as many as 7,000 copies. As you can imagine, these copiers require frequent service and repair. Therefore, we are considering a service and repair contract, and your firm has been highly recommended to us.

We'd like an estimate of your monthly fees.

If you need more information, please give me a call. If you'd like to see our operation before you give me a quote, please call for an appointment.

Sincerely,

Alternative Phrases:

- The machines average 7,000 copies a day and require frequent service and repair.
- You can stop by during normal business hours if you'd like to see our operation before you submit a bid.

CHANGING STANDING ORDER FOR COPIER SUPPLIES

Dear Ms. Ross:

We need to increase our standing order for bond copies paper and toner. As your records show, you currently deliver supplies for 10,000 copies each month. For the last two months, we've had to call you for an additional delivery.

Starting next month, please deliver supplies for 15,000 copies, and bill us in the usual manner.

Thanks so much for your help.

Sincerely,

EXPLAINING A PROBLEM WITH COPIER SERVICE

Dear Mr. Ocaboc:

As your records will show, we purchased a Kodak 1700 copier and a service contract from you in January of this year. About 30 days ago, we began having trouble, and although your service representative has been quick to respond, the repairs don't last.

What happens is this: After running about 100 copies, the image begins to fade. We've discovered we need to keep the toner bin absolutely full. According to the instruction book and your service rep, we shouldn't get such fading until the machine is almost out of toner. Physically jiggling the toner bin will get us through another 50 to 75 copies, but such action shouldn't be necessary.

Your service rep has replaced the bin and made several adjustments, but to no avail. Typically, after a visit we can run copies for about two days—roughly 500 copies—before we begin to have problems.

Obviously, something is wrong! At this point, we feel replacing the machine is probably the best answer. Something needs to be changed, and quickly, for the current situation is intolerable.

Please call me this week so that we can determine exactly how the replacement will take place.

Sincerely,

Alternative Phrases:

- As your records show . . . and a service contract from your company in January of this year.
- Something needs to be changed, and quickly, for the current situation is inconvenient.
- We feel our only choice is to insist on a replacement machine.
- Unless you can guarantee that a repair will cause no more problems, we are going to insist on a replacement unit.
- We are unwilling to continue using this machine and expect a replacement.

CANCELING WATER DELIVERY

Dear Sir/Madam:

We have decided to switch from bottled water to an in-line water filter and, as a result, want to cancel our weekly water delivery. Please pick up your water cooler and any leftover water on the next delivery date. We will pay the final bill upon receipt.

Sincerely,

Alternative Phrase:

- Please call me for an appointment.

ASKING FOR A CHANGE IN COFFEE SERVICE

Dear Bob:

Our customer traffic is increasing, and that means we need more coffee! Currently, we're receiving coffee and associated supplies to serve about

100 cups a week. Please increase our order so that we can serve about 150 cups a week, and bill us in the usual manner.

By the way, I'd like you to know we get lots of compliments on your coffee. Obviously, you're doing something right!

Sincerely,

Alternative Phrase:

- Would you let me know what it would cost to increase our supplies to serve 150 cups each week?

DETAILING A COMPUTER PROBLEM

Dear Mr. Sperry:

As we discussed on the phone, we are still having trouble with one of our IBM clones. You asked me to detail the problem in writing, so that you could determine what needs to be done. Here is my understanding of what actually happens:

1. Whenever anyone turns on the computer and the printer at the beginning of the day, using the master switch on the power surge unit, everything appears normal—that is, the computer comes on, the date and time are displayed properly, and we're able to begin working either with the word processor (WordStar 3.1) or the spreadsheet (VP Planner).
2. Work proceeds in a normal fashion, including printing—at least for a while.
3. Then, in an apparently random fashion, the computer will leave the program and return us to the DOS prompt (A). When this happens, the file we were working on just disappears. This may happen several times.

I can find no pattern. As you suggested, I've kept a tally during the last four days, and the score looks like this: We've been returned to DOS twice while we were using WordStar and three times while we were using VP Planner. Once it happened when we asked VP to print a spreadsheet, but when we created that same spreadsheet again, we were able to print it with no problems. During this period, WordStar printed normally, but I know we've also been returned to DOS while printing with WordStar.

You also asked me to check on the electrical circuit. According to the building manager, the computer we're having problems with is on the same circuit as another computer which has the same programs and gets roughly the same amount and type of work. Yet the second computer is doing just fine, so I doubt if it's the electricity.

Mike Wilder, an engineer here who has an Apple at home, suggested we might have a weak chip in the problem computer. I gather he's saying that one of the chips may be more sensitive to changes in power than it should be. I have no idea if that makes sense, or, if it does, what to do about it.

We've been forced to limit the use of the problem computer to minor projects only, which is unacceptable.

Please give me a call as soon as possible so that we can figure out what to do.

Sincerely,

Alternative Phrases:

- I'd like to have you come to our office and work with the computer. Perhaps you can spot something I haven't. Would you please give me a call so that we can set a time?
- I think the next thing to do is to bring the computer to you.
- Obviously, this can't go on, so we have decided the only acceptable solution is a replacement CPU. Please give me a call and tell me when we can expect the new unit.

DETAILING A RECEIPT OF AN INCOMPLETE ORDER

Dear Jonathan:

Enclosed is a copy of the order we sent you on February 13. Yesterday, we received most of our books, together with an invoice indicating the proper items had been shipped. However, the quantities we received match neither the invoice nor our original order. The following items were missing from this shipment:

2 copies of *Mommy, I Hurt* by Sutherland

1 copy of *What You Think of Me Is None of My Business* by Whittaker

5 copies of *Single Parent Solutions* by Wayman

We'd like the missing books as soon as possible, since all are selling well. If they've been back-ordered, I'd appreciate a phone call letting me know when to expect them.

Sincerely,

Alternative Phrases:

- Please ship the missing books at once.
- This is not the first time we've had problems getting our order filled properly by your company. We'd like to continue doing business with you, but unless there are some changes, we'll be forced to fill our orders elsewhere.

LETTERS DEALING WITH EMPLOYMENT AND EMPLOYEES

TO JOB APPLICANT REQUESTING MORE INFORMATION

Dear Ms. Greene:

Thank you very much for your application for our editorial position. Your tear sheets and credits are impressive.

Before we schedule an interview, we'd like to check your references. Please call me with the names and phone numbers of three or four people you've worked with in an editorial capacity.

Sincerely,

Alternative Phrases:

- We were pleased to receive your application for the editorial position.
- Your application for our editorial position impressed us, and we'd like to talk with you. Please call us to arrange an interview.
- Please send me the names and phone numbers of some people you've worked with whom I can talk to.

TO JOB APPLICANT REQUESTING AN ADDITIONAL FORM BE FILLED OUT

Dear Mr. Miller:

We're impressed with the résumé you sent in response to our ad for a CPA, and we'd like you to complete the enclosed form. We know from experience that this form will provide us with the information we need to continue our screening process. Assuming that we receive the form by the end of the week and that the information provided on it is in order, we will be setting up interviews by the end of the month. We will be in touch with you by then.

Yours truly,

Alternative Phrases:

- Thank you for your résumé; your credentials appear excellent. The next step is for you to complete the enclosed form.
- We will use the completed form to complete our screening process.
- The interviewing process will begin toward the end of the month. You can expect to hear from us by then.

TO JOB APPLICANT—"WE'LL BE IN TOUCH"

Dear Mr. Gleason:

Thank you for your application for our systems manager position. Your qualifications appear suitable, and we are now checking your references. If that goes well, I'll call you next week to schedule an interview.

Sincerely,

Alternative Phrase:

- We received your application for our systems manager position and are now in the process of checking your references. Please give me a call next week so that I can tell you the status of your application.

TO JOB APPLICANT STATING THE JOB HAS BEEN FILLED

Dear Mr. Jones:

Thank you for your application for our bookkeeping position. We have filled the job, but were impressed with your résumé and will keep it on file in case another position opens up.

Sincerely,

Alternative Phrases:

- Although we have filled our bookkeeping job, your résumé indicates you have excellent qualifications. We will keep it on file.
- We regret to inform you that we have chosen another applicant for our bookkeeping position. Thank you for your application.

TO JOB APPLICANT WHO DOES NOT MEET QUALIFICATIONS

Dear Mr. Coy:

Thank you for your interest in our environmental testing department. Unfortunately, we are not able to provide much training and therefore must insist on both a degree and a minimum of five years practical experience.

Sincerely,

CHECKING AN EMPLOYMENT REFERENCE

Dear Mr. Enright:

Mr. Roger Gleason has given us your name as a reference as a former employer. We are considering hiring him to help us with systems management.

Please call, collect if you wish, or respond in writing with any information which might help us in our decision.

Thank you for your assistance.

Sincerely,

Alternative Phrases:

- Roger Gleason suggested we get in touch with you.
- Mr. Roger Gleason is a candidate for an assistant systems management position with our firm, and he's given us your name as a reference.
- Enclosed is a reference form we'd like you to complete and return to us.

CHECKING A PERSONAL REFERENCE

Dear Ms. Wilder:

Ms. Karen James has given us your name as a personal reference. We understand you and Ms. James were roommates during college. She has applied for a sales position with us, and we would appreciate any pertinent information you could give us.

You may call me, collect, at the number below, or write me a letter. Your response will, of course, be held in strictest confidence.

Sincerely,

Alternative Phrases:

- Karen James has applied for a sales job with our firm and has given us your name as a personal reference. Could you tell us a little bit about her?
- Please call me, collect, at the number below.

REFERENCE FOR FORMER EMPLOYEE

Dear Mr. Sindicich:

I'm delighted to heartily recommend Ms. Kathy Price as a legal secretary. She came to us immediately after she had completed her secretarial course and was with us five years. As she probably told you, she left only because her husband was transferred to your city. We were truly sorry to see her go; not only was she an excellent secretary, but we felt would also make an excellent para-legal. We would have encouraged her to continue her education with that in mind.

She has an excellent mind, is quick to grasp the complexities of the law, and had an outstanding performance and attendance record.

Sincerely,

Alternative Phrases:

- I am pleased to recommend Ms. Kathy Price as a legal secretary.
- Mrs. Kathy Price gave us excellent service as a legal secretary for five years.
- It was difficult to find an adequate replacement when she left.

WELCOME TO NEW EMPLOYEE

Dear New Employee:

Congratulations on your new position with our company. We're glad to have you as part of our team.

Your supervisor will give you a "New Employee's Packet." In it you will find information about parking, hours, a map of the plant, and an overview of our benefits plan.

Please feel free to ask questions as you learn your way around.

Sincerely,

Alternative Phrases:

- Welcome to our company. We're looking forward to working with you.
- If you have questions, please direct them to your supervisor.

ORIENTATION FOR NEW EMPLOYEE

Dear Ms. Smith:

Welcome to Beta Computer Products. Congratulations on your new position in product development.

There are a few general things you should know about our company:

- Parking is provided, but you'll need a permit. On your first day, simply give your name to the guard who will assign you a temporary space.
- Our working hours are from 7:00 A.M. to 5:00 P.M., with lunch between 11:30 and 12:30, Monday through Thursday. On Friday we start at 7:00 A.M. and quit at 11:00 A.M.
- Each new employee needs to check in with reception until issued a badge. Just give your name to the receptionist, who will issue you a temporary pass.
- Your supervisor's name is Barbara Bender and can be found in Building 3. The receptionist will tell you exactly how to get there.

Ms. Bender will provide you with all the necessary forms, including those you need to receive your permanent parking sticker and permanent badge. She will also show you exactly where you'll be working and get you started.

I will bring a copy of our benefits package to you sometime during your second week. I look forward to meeting you then.

Sincerely,

Alternative Phrases:

- Here is some information that should make it easier for you to get oriented:
- Enclosed is your parking permit. It should be placed on the left side of the front windshield where the guard can see it as you enter the lot.
- As you might expect, there is some information we will need from you. Your supervisor will provide you with the necessary forms. Please fill them out and return them to your supervisor during your first week with us.

EXPLANATION OF BENEFIT PLAN

Dear Mr. Baker:

As you remember, our Employee Benefit Plan has been designed to provide benefits for employees who have been employed with us for at least 90 days. You will be eligible to participate on June 21. You may choose all or some of the following benefits:

Medical Insurance Plan

You will become eligible for medical insurance on June 21.

The *Medical Insurance Plan* is paid for entirely by the company. It includes such features as:

- Annual preventive examinations for you and your dependents.
- Hospitalization. Paid at 80 percent of the actual cost up to $250,000 after you pay a $250 deductible for each covered person annually.

The details of the plan are in the enclosed brochure, "Medical Plan." To enroll, simply fill out the form attached to the brochure and return it to me. Coverage will begin fifteen days after I receive the completed form.

The *Dental Insurance Plan* is partially paid for by the company. It includes such features as:

- Annual cleaning and diagnostic services. Paid at 100 percent of customary charges.
- Basic services, such as cavity filling. Paid at 75 percent of customary charges for you and 50 percent for any dependents.
- Emergency services not to exceed $500 annually for each covered person.

The details of the plan are in the enclosed brochure, "Dental Plan." To enroll, simply fill out the form attached to the brochure and return it to me. Coverage will begin forty-five days after I receive the completed form.

The *Pension Plan* is also partially paid for by the company. The benefits and costs are dependent on your length of employment and salary classification. I've included a chart that makes this clear. As you can see, some vesting occurs as early as the completion of your third year with us.

The details of the plan are in the enclosed brochure, "Pension Plan." You will be eligible for participation after 180 days of continuous employment. To enroll, simply fill out the form attached to the brochure and return it to me. Participation will begin 30 days after I receive the completed form.

I'll be happy to answer any questions you might have.

Sincerely,

Alternative Phrases:

- You have now been with our firm for 90 days, which means you are eligible to participate in our employee benefit plans.
- Please make your selections and return the forms to me as soon as possible.
- The Pension Plan is fully paid for by the company.

EXPLANATION OF PENSION PLAN

Dear Ms. Barros:

Your pension benefits are determined by a formula taking into consideration three factors:

1. The number of years you work for us.
2. Your Final Average Earnings (FAE) over that period.
3. The amount of your primary Social Security benefits.

Provided you have worked at least ten years for the company, you will receive a minimum of $175.00 per month.

Your FAE is based on your highest average earnings during 60 consecutive months out of the final 120 months.

The offset of Social Security and other primary government benefits is a flat 45 percent.

The attached chart will allow you to roughly determine your benefits. If you need specific information, or have any other questions, please contact me.

Sincerely,

Alternative Phrases:

- You are approaching your ten-year anniversary with our firm which means it's time to review our pension plan.
- The following information will give you an overview of our pension plan:

TO EMPLOYEE APPROACHING RETIREMENT

Dear Ms. Bragg:

Congratulations on your upcoming retirement. As you know, you're entitled to certain benefits as the result of your tenure with us. You probably have some questions, and I'd be happy to go over your retirement plan with you so you'll know exactly what to expect.

Please give me a call at extension 142 to set up an appointment.

Sincerely,

EXPLAINING NEW HOLIDAY SCHEDULE

Dear Ms. Blanchard:

Starting July 1, our company will provide the following paid holidays:

Independence Day
Labor Day
Thanksgiving Day
Thanksgiving Friday
Christmas Eve (half day)
Christmas Day
Memorial Day

Sincerely,

Alternative Phrases:

- As you know, there have been some changes in our holiday schedule.
- Please keep this letter or mark these holidays on your calendar.

TO EMPLOYMENT AGENCY REGARDING FEES

Dear Ms. Sweeny:

We are expanding our offices, which means that in the next few months we'll have to hire several people. Although we usually use the classifieds when we need new people, we realize that an agency could help us do the screening.

Therefore, I'd like information on (1) how you find your candidates; (2) how you screen them; (3) what your fees are; and (4) your fee payment policies.

Thank you for your help.

Sincerely,

Alternative Phrases:

- Due to the expansion of our business, we anticipate that we will need to hire at least five additional people.
- Because we need five additional people, we realize we could use some help with the screening process.
- I am, of course, interested in any other information you feel I should have about your firm.

ASKING ABOUT CONVERTING TEMPORARY HELP TO PERMANENT HELP

Dear Ms. Quinlan:

Annie Jeffries has become such an integral part of our operation that we'd like to change her employment from temporary to permanent. I know this means we have an obligation to your agency, but frankly, after reading the contract, I can't quite figure it out.

Annie began as a word processor. Now she's doing all sorts of things, including some training, some systems work, and even some development work. Please let me know how to proceed.

Sincerely,

Alternative Phrases:

- We'd like to convert Annie Jeffries from a temporary employee to a permanent employee. Could you tell me how to proceed?

- What, exactly, do we need to do to start and complete this process?
- Please give me a call so that we can begin this process.

COMPLAINT ABOUT TEMPORARY EMPLOYEE

Dear Mr. Bolton:

Something has to be done about Judy Fixx, the word processor you sent us this week. Although her computer skills seem adequate, her attitude is causing problems. For example, she seems to resent being asked to make corrections, and she often turns out very poor work.

Perhaps you can have a word with her, or perhaps it would be best to replace her. As you know, this project is really under the gun, and we don't have time to coddle anyone.

Please let me know what you plan to do.

Sincerely,

Alternative Phrases:

- We are having problems with your temp, Judy Fixx.
- Judy Fixx, the temporary word processor from your firm, is not working out.
- We're probably going to have to ask you to replace the temporary word processor you sent us, Ms. Judy Fixx.

COMPLAINT ABOUT TEMPORARY EMPLOYMENT SERVICE

Dear Larry:

What's happened? The last three production workers you sent us have not been able, or willing, to perform to our standards. Have you changed your interview and testing standards? Or are we not being clear about what we want?

Please give me a call so that we can straighten this out.

Yours truly,

Alternative Phrases:

- We have had problems with the last three production workers you sent us.
- As you know, we've done business with your firm for several years—to our mutual satisfaction. However, the last three production workers you've sent us haven't worked out.
- If we can't find a way to improve the quality of the people you're sending us, we'll have to find another agency.

DECLINING EMPLOYMENT OFFER

Dear Mr. Wall:

Thank you so much for your willingness to hire me as sales manager. I have, however, decided on another position.

I appreciate your time and interest.

Sincerely,

Alternative Phrases:

- I was pleased that you offered me the job of sales manager.
- After careful consideration, I have chosen a position with another firm.
- I enjoyed talking with you and trust all goes well for you and your company.

ACCEPTING EMPLOYMENT OFFER

Dear Mr. Wall:

Thank you so much for your willingness to hire me as sales manager. I am delighted to accept. I should be established in Ohio by the end of the month, which means I can start on Monday, September 21.

Enclosed is my signed copy of our employment agreement.

I'm looking forward to a long and profitable mutual association.

Sincerely,

Alternative Phrases:

- I am pleased to accept your offer to make me your sales manager.
- It should take me no longer than the end of the month to locate and move into an apartment in Cleveland, so you can expect me on Monday morning, September 21.
- My signed copy of the employment agreement is enclosed.
- I feel this is the beginning of a mutually profitable venture.

INVITATIONS TO BUSINESS SOCIAL FUNCTIONS

Invitations can be formal or informal, depending on the type of party. The easiest type of invitation is probably the kind you pick up at a stationery store where you simply fill in the appropriate blanks. If you have graphics on your computer—and the time and inclination—you can create your own "standard" invitation. Invitations can also be issued in letter form, and informal invitations may often be simply handwritten.

But whatever form your invitation takes, be clear about exactly whom you're inviting. If it's the whole staff, say so; if it's only the officers, it's probably better to issue individual invitations.

INFORMAL LETTER INVITATION

Dear Team Members,

We're having a party! We're celebrating our record profits for the quarter, and we'd like to invite our whole staff to join us on Friday, July 14, between 4 and 7 P.M.

We'll provide some snacks and a no-host bar.

Give me a call Thursday morning to let me know about how many will attend.

Sincerely,

Alternative Phrases:

- It's time to celebrate!
- Please come, and bring your whole staff, to help us celebrate.

FORMAL LETTER INVITATION

Dear Mr. and Mrs. Peterson,

We are pleased to invite you to our official opening at our new location on August 8 at 8:00 P.M.

R.S.V.P. by August 5.

Sincerely,

Alternative Phrase:

- It is with great pleasure that we invite you to . . .

DECLINING AN INVITATION—INFORMAL

Dear Alan,

Thanks so much for your invitation to join you at your opening on August 8. Unfortunately, I have a prior commitment that evening.

I know I would have enjoyed the gala introduction to your new quarters. You can be sure I'll drop in to see you soon.

As ever,

Alternative Phrases:

- I'm sorry, but I will be out of town that whole week.
- I would have been delighted to attend, but my schedule simply won't permit it.
- I'm looking forward to stopping by and seeing what you're doing.

DECLINING AN INVITATION—FORMAL

Dear Ms. Bush:

It is with genuine regret that my wife and I must decline your kind invitation to the opening of your new gallery on August 8.

Be assured that we both wish you the very best and expect to stop by for a look before long.

Sincerely,

Alternative Phrases:

- I am sorry that neither my wife nor I will be able to attend your opening on (appropriate date).
- Please accept my regrets for your opening on August 8.
- We certainly wish you the best with your new venture.

LETTERS CONCERNING SUBSCRIPTIONS

REQUESTING A COMPLIMENTARY SUBSCRIPTION

Dear Sir/Madam:

You may be aware that not only are we OEM's designing peripheral for IBM and IBM clones, but that we advertise at least six times each year with you. Of course, we receive copies of *PC World* when our ad appears, but we'd like a complimentary subscription to your magazine so that we can stay current even when we're not advertising.

Sincerely,

Alternative Phrases:

- Since we are constantly working on developing new products, and advertise with you at least six times a year, we'd like a complimentary subscription.
- It seems to us our news value and our frequency of advertising would entitle us to a complimentary subscription.

CANCELING A SUBSCRIPTION

Dear Sir/Madam:

Please cancel our subscription to *MicroTimes* with the September, 1991 issue. Since we're dropping our line of computer products, we will no longer need your magazine.

Please pro-rate our subscription fee and return the balance.

I've attached a copy of the mailing label, which indicates our subscription is due to expire with the July, 1992 issue.

Sincerely,

Alternative Phrases:

- Please cancel our subscription to *MicroTimes.* Our mailing label is attached below.
- Enclosed is our mailing label. We'd like to cancel our subscription and receive the balance of our subscription fee.

THANKS FOR SPECIAL SERVICES

Dear Mary:

I wanted to thank you and your crew for the extra attention you gave our offices before and after our Five-Year Anniversary Celebration last weekend.

Not only did you do your usual good job, but you also went the extra mile, and it was appreciated. The flowers were a delightful surprise, and your willingness to clean again early Monday morning allowed us to open our doors for regular business in fine fashion.

Thanks again for your continuing excellent service.

Sincerely,

Alternative Phrases:

- Thanks so much to you and your crew for the extra . . .
- It was such a pleasure to walk into our offices after our party that I wanted to thank you and your crew . . .
- We really appreciate your excellent service.

ERROR IN PROMOTIONAL MATERIAL

Dear Robin:

Somehow or other the special flier we sent telling you of our new address had the wrong telephone number! A real case of Murphy's Law in operation.

Our *real* new phone number is (213) 555-7789.

We're truly sorry for the inconvenience and trust you'll make a note of the correction.

Sincerely,

Alternative Phrases:

- Please forgive us. The flier we recently sent you had the wrong phone number.
- The flier we sent you informing you of our new address and phone number had the wrong number.

TRAVEL ARRANGEMENTS

ENCLOSING AN ITINERARY

Dear Mr. Elsworth:

Our president, Mr. Brian Hensley, asked me to send you a copy of his itinerary during his across-the-country visits to our stores.

On the enclosed schedule, you'll find the address, phone number, and manager's name listed under the appropriate date. Following that information, I've also listed the hotel and hotel number where he will be staying each night.

As you know, these schedules are tentative at best, so you may want to check with me before making any long distance calls.

Sincerely,

Alternative Phrases:

- Enclosed is the itinerary Mr. Brian Hensley will be following during his cross-country store visits.
- The attached itinerary shows Mr. Hensley's schedule during his annual cross-country visits to our stores.
- If there are changes during the trip, I'll have the information. Give me a call if you need it.

CONFIRMING AN APPOINTMENT AT A HOTEL

Dear Ms. Ackerman:

Janice Lynch asked me to drop you a line confirming your appointment with her at the Hyatt-Regency Hotel, Embaradero Center, San Francisco, on May 17 at 10:30 A.M.

She's looking forward to meeting you then.

Yours very truly,

Alternative Phrases:

- Miss Lynch asked me to contact you to confirm . . .
- This will confirm your appointment with Janice Lynch at . . .

CONFIRMING HOTEL RESERVATIONS

Dear Ms. Collins:

This is to confirm my reservation at the Hotel Clarion for Tuesday, September 12 to Saturday, September 16, 19––. I expect to arrive at the hotel at about 3:00 P.M. on September 12.

Please bill my advance reservation deposit to my credit card account (type of card, number and expiration date).

Sincerely,

Alternative Phrases:

- Thanks so much for your help in getting . . .
- My reservations are finally firm.
- At present, I expect to be in your city from (day, date) to (day, date).

TRANSMITTAL LETTERS

Dear Mr. Guenther:

Enclosed is a copy of the diskette we'd like duplicated. We'd like 500 copies on your Vanilla Wafer, each in its own white envelope. We will provide and apply our own labels.

Thanks so much for your help. If you have any questions, give me a call.

Sincerely,

Alternative Phrases:

- We're ready to have version 2.5 duplicated for distribution.
- Please make 500 copies using your Vanilla Wafer disk, and put each in its own white envelope.
- The labels are being printed now, and we'll apply them ourselves.
- We appreciate your service. I assume you'll call if you have any questions.

FLOPPY DISK IN SEPARATE PACKAGE

Dear Jeff:

Because of the delay, we've arranged for our programmer to send you the disk for duplication from New Jersey. We'd like 500 copies on your

Vanilla Wafer, each in its own white envelope. Enclosed is the camera-ready art for the labels, which we'd like you to apply.

When the disks are ready, give me a call, and I'll come to your plant to pick them up.

Sincerely,

Alternative Phrases:

- Since we've gotten behind schedule, our programmer will send you the master disk from New Jersey.
- Please put a label on each disk; camera-ready art is enclosed.
- I'd like to pick the disks up as soon as they're finished, so give me a call when they're ready.

INFORMATION ENCLOSED

Dear Ms. Jenks:

Enclosed is the packet of information you requested. It's self-explanatory, and an order blank and discount coupon are enclosed.

Thank you for your interest,

Alternative Phrases:

- The enclosed packet contains the information you requested.
- I think you'll find all your questions are answered, and there's an order blank on the last page.
- We're delighted with your interest. If you have any questions, don't hesitate to call.

DOCUMENTS REQUIRING SIGNATURE ENCLOSED

Dear Ms. Davis:

Enclosed are the contracts for the work to be performed by my client. Please sign and return all copies to me. I will then get the balance of the signatures and return an executed copy to you.

Sincerely,

Alternative Phrases:

- Here are your contracts for . . .
- Once you've signed all five copies, return them to me.
- As soon as I get the rest of the signatures, I'll send you a copy of the executed agreement.
- I think everything is clear, but if you have any questions please call.

DOCUMENTS REQUIRING SIGNATURE TO FOLLOW

Dear Anne:

Alexis Properties, Inc., tells me they put the contracts in the mail directly to you today. When you get them, please look them over carefully. If you have any questions, give me a call. After you sign them, send them directly to me, and I'll double check them. I will keep your copy on file here as usual.

Congratulations!

Alternative Phrases:

- I talked with Alexis Properties, Inc., today and they said they had sent the contracts to you.
- Be sure you read them carefully—if there's anything you don't understand, give me a call.
- Send them to me once you've signed them. I'll make sure everything is OK and then send them on to the publisher.

Chapter 2

WRITING LETTERS ABOUT MONEY

COLLECTION LETTERS

PAYMENT LETTERS

CORRECTING BILLING AND BANKING ERRORS

LETTERS ABOUT CREDIT

LETTERS ABOUT DONATIONS

Enclosing a Donation to a Worthy Cause—With a Quotable Statement
Refusing to Donate to a Worthy Cause
Postponing a Donation to a Worthy Cause
Reminder of Pledge
Special Fundraising

Business deals with money all the time, and secretaries, because they are an integral part of any business, must be able to write letters about money. Dealing with money matters on behalf of your firm requires delicate handling—people are sensitive about money. Because of this, your letters must be crisp, clear, and as neutral as possible.

SECRETARY'S TIPS ON WRITING LETTERS ABOUT MONEY

1. *Be sure you understand the purpose of the letter.* Clarity of purpose is more important than ever when writing letters about money. For example, are you trying to collect? Or sending money? Or straightening out confusion? Maybe establishing credit? Or negotiating or renegotiating a contract? Whatever the purpose, you must be able to state it clearly and simply.
2. *Get all the information you need before composing the letter.* When writing letters about money, you not only need to know the exact dollar amounts, you also need to have all the supporting information about how those dollar amounts were arrived at. Sometimes you'll need to include the supporting information; often, however, you simply need the background in order to generate the letter.
3. *Determine the tone of the letter.* The tone of letters dealing with money is all important. Some letters can be informal, while others must take on a firm, formal tone. The specific situation will determine the tone you use. But whatever the case, avoid, if possible, putting the recipient of the letter on the defensive.

   Give serious thought about who the "author" of the letter should be. For example, if your job description includes bookkeeping, it may be best if you use that title. Moreover, many letters dealing with money should be signed by someone who is perceived to have more authority than a secretary.

4. *The first paragraph should contain the most important information.* Get to the point quickly so that the recipient knows exactly what the letter is about. If you're enclosing a check, say so. Specify the amount, and state why you're sending it. If you're asking for money, make it clear exactly how much you're asking for and why you're making the request. Supporting information, if it's required at all, then follows in its order of importance.
5. *Make it clear what response, if any, is expected from the reader.* Let the recipient of the letter know exactly what sort of action is necessary. If your account needs to be credited, say so. If you're expecting a check, spell out the date you expect to receive it. If you need confirmation of an order, tell the reader how you want to receive that confirmation and when.
6. *Be concise and complete.* Because money is a sensitive subject, it's easy to say more in a letter than need be said. So be concise. In addition, double check your letters about money to be sure they give the recipient all the necessary information. Be sure the figures you use are correct; if you've gotten the figures from someone else, run them through your calculator to make sure there are no errors.

COLLECTION LETTERS

ASKING FOR PAYMENT OF AN ACCOUNT

Dear Mr. Dody:

Our records show it's been over 60 days since we've received a payment on your account. The total balance due is $257.48. In order to bring your account current, we need to receive $128.74 by July 5.

Thank you for your cooperation. If you have any questions or need additional information, please give me a call.

Sincerely,

Alternative Phrases:

- According to our records . . .
- We have not received a payment from you for over . . .
- We expect payment immediately.

ASKING FOR PAYMENT, SUGGESTING A PAYMENT PLAN

Dear Mr. Benet:

As I'm sure you're aware, your account with us is past due. Our records indicate your balance is now $1,380.00 and we haven't received a payment in over two months.

When this matter was brought to my attention, it occurred to me that a schedule of payments might be helpful. Therefore, my suggestion is that you send us the money due in the following way:

May 1 . . . $690.00
June 1 . . . $345.00
July 2 . . . $345.00

If this is agreeable, simply send us the first payment by May 1. Should you have any questions, please give me a call.

If we haven't heard from you by May 1, I will be forced to turn this account over to our collection agency. If this happens, interest will be added to the original amount, and the transaction will be reflected on your credit rating.

Sincerely yours,

Alternative Phrases:

- Are you aware that your account with us is past due?
- According to our records your balance . . .
- Since the amount is large, it's occurred to me that a payment schedule might be helpful. I suggest the following:
- On May 1, I will be forced to turn your account over to our collection agency unless I've heard from you.

SERIES OF THREE COLLECTION LETTERS

When you write collection letters, keep in mind that your first letter should be framed as a reminder, because you want to keep the customer. Subsequent letters may take on a more forceful tone. The three letters in this series illustrate this progression.

1.

Dear Ms. Pickering:

You may have overlooked sending us your monthly payment of $75.00, which was due July 1.

We would appreciate your prompt payment so that we can bring your account up to date.

If you've already sent your payment, please disregard this letter.

Sincerely,

Alternative Phrases:

- Did you forget to send us . . . ?
- Have you overlooked sending us . . . ?
- Please send your payment immediately so that we may bring your account up to date.

2.

Dear Ms. Pickering:

Your account with us is now seriously overdue. It has been 60 days since we've received a payment, and 30 days since we sent you the first reminder. The total due is now $625.00.

If there is a problem, and you can't bring your account current, I'd be happy to discuss it with you. You may give me a call, collect. Otherwise, we'll expect the total amount due no later than August 31.

Sincerely,

Alternative Phrases:

- Are you aware that your account with us is now seriously past due?
- I'd be willing to talk with you about your account if you have a problem bringing it current.

3.

Dear Ms. Pickering:

We have not received a payment from you for 90 days, nor have we received any communication about your account. The total due is now $625.00.

Unfortunately, our next step is to turn your account over to a collection agency. If we're forced to do that, the collection will appear on your credit history, making it difficult for you to arrange credit in the future.

Before we do turn your account over to a collection agency, I'd like to discuss your account with you. We are willing to work with you to get this matter straightened out. You may call me collect.

However, if we don't receive payment or hear from you by close of business on September 15, we will be forced to turn your account over to a collection agency. The matter will then be out of our hands.

Please get in touch with me.

Sincerely,

Alternative Phrases:

- In spite of our willingness to cooperate with you and in spite of sending you several notices, we have not received payment from you.
- We really don't want to turn this account over to our collection agency, but we may be forced to do so. A negative report will appear . . .
- Please give me a chance to talk with you before I turn your account over to a collection agency.

CHANGING PAYMENT SCHEDULE FOR A CUSTOMER

Dear Ms. Pickering:

Thank you for your telephone call. As we discussed, we can change your payment schedule as follows:

1. We will extend your contract an additional nine months.
2. This will reduce your monthly payments from $72.50 to $50.00.
3. We will change the monthly due date from the first of each month to the twentieth, starting next month.

I will expect your first payment on this new schedule on or before September 20. I've enclosed a new payment schedule that reflects these arrangements.

Thank you for your cooperation.

Sincerely,

Alternative Phrases:

- I'm glad you called to discuss your payment schedule. We can arrange to change it as follows:
- Your first payment per this new schedule must arrive on or before September 20 for this arrangement to take effect.
- We appreciate your cooperation.

REQUESTING PAYMENT OF A PERSONAL LOAN

Depending on the relationship, you may want to hand write letter requesting payment of a personal loan.

1.

Dear Rachel,

It's time I collected the $500.00 I lent you several months ago. Ideally, I'd like to get the whole amount, but I recognize that may not be possible. If not, could we agree that you will send me $100.00 the first of each month starting next month?

Please let me know just what to expect.

Regards,

Alternative Phrases:

- I need to collect the $500.00 I lent you . . .
- Please send me the $500.00 I lent you . . . If the full amount is not possible, could we agree . . . ?
- Give me a call if this isn't satisfactory.

2.

Dear Dick,

What do you want to do about the $500 you owe me? I know it's been a rough time for you—I understand. Please drop me a note, or better yet, give me a call, and let me know what's happening.

Sincerely,

Alternative Phrases:

- How do you want to handle the $500.00 I lent you?
- I know you've had a rough time and I do understand, but I'd like to get this worked out.
- Give me a call and let me know what you're able to do.

REQUESTING PAYMENT OF A PERSONAL LOAN ON BEHALF OF SOMEONE ELSE

Dear Ms. McDonald:

Peter Simms has asked me to drop you this note to let you know he feels it's time you repaid the $500.00 he lent you several months ago. He'd like me to tell you he'd appreciate payment in full, but recognizes this may not be possible.

As an alternative, he suggests you begin making payments of $100.00 on the first of each month starting next month.

If this isn't agreeable, please give him a call to discuss the situation. Otherwise, he will expect your check on the first.

Sincerely,

Alternative Phrases:

- I'm writing on behalf of Peter Simms who has asked me . . .
- Perhaps you could make five monthly payments of $100.00 each starting the first of next month.
- Mr. Simms will expect a check on the first unless he hears otherwise.

ABOUT MISSING ENCLOSURE OF MONEY

Dear Mr. Thompson:

We received your letter stating that you were enclosing your check for $750.00, which, as you stated, would bring your account current. However, we found no check in the envelope.

Please send the check as soon as possible so that we can properly credit your account.

Sincerely,

Alternative Phrases:

- I'm sure you will be as surprised as I was when I tell you your check for $750.00 was not in your letter. You are correct, that amount would bring your account current.
- I will look for your check soon.

ABOUT MISSING SIGNATURE ON A CHECK

Dear Mr. Thompson:

Thank you for your check of $750.00. However, since it was unsigned, I am returning it to you for your signature.

When we receive a signed check in this amount we will credit your account.

Sincerely,

Alternative Phrases:

- The check you sent us is lacking a signature. I am returning it so you can sign it.
- We will credit your account as soon as we receive a signed check.

ABOUT RECEIPT OF NSF CHECK

Dear Mr. Goldstone:

Enclosed is your January rent check which was returned to us marked Non-Sufficient Funds. Please send us either a money order or a cashier's check to replace the funds.

Sincerely,

Alternative Phrases:

- The January rent check you sent us was returned by your bank marked Non-Sufficient Funds.
- Since your January rent check was returned unpaid by your bank, we must insist on replacement by money order or cashier's check.
- Because your last rent check was returned unpaid, we must insist that it be replaced with a money order or cashier's check. We will return the unpaid check to you as soon as we receive its replacement.

PAYMENT LETTERS

SENDING TOTAL LATE PAYMENT

Dear Ms. Lanski:

Thank you for your offer to allow us to pay our past due balance over a period of three months. I am delighted to tell you that this won't be necessary and am enclosing a check for $345.87.

Thank you again for your understanding in this matter.

Sincerely,

Alternative Phrases:

- We appreciate the opportunity to pay our past due balance over a three-month period.
- Instead of paying our past due balance over three months as you suggested, I am enclosing a check for the total amount.
- I appreciate your willingness to work with me.

SENDING PARTIAL PAYMENT

Dear Ms. Youngerman:

I know our firm owes you $500.00 as of today, but because of collection problems at this end, I am unable to make payment in full. Enclosed is our check for $250.00. We expect to be able to pay the balance within ten working days, but will let you know by phone if that won't be possible.

Thank you for your consideration.

Sincerely yours,

Alternative Phrases:

- Because of temporary difficulties, I am enclosing a partial payment on our account.
- You will have the balance no later than May 15.
- I appreciate your cooperation.

SENDING PARTIAL LATE PAYMENT

Dear Ms. Lanski:

Enclosed is our check for $200.00, which, according to our records, leaves a balance due you of $145.87. I know this still leaves our account in a "past-due" position, but I expect to be able to send you the balance within two weeks.

Thank you for your understanding and cooperation.

Sincerely,

Alternative Phrases:

- The enclosed $200.00 check will reduce our past due balance to $145.87. I will send you the balance by the end of the month.
- I appreciate your cooperation.

ASKING FOR TIME EXTENSION ON PAYMENT DUE

Dear Ms. Youngerman:

Our firm's payment to you of $500.00 is due at the end of next week. We regret that we will be unable to meet that deadline. We expect to be able to send you the total amount on July 21 and will let you know if there will be any change.

Thank you for your cooperation.

Sincerely yours,

Alternative Phrases:

- We will be unable to pay you the $500.00 on the due date. We expect to be able to send . . .
- I will send you the total amount . . .
- I appreciate your understanding.

TO BANK EXPLAINING WHY A PAYMENT WILL BE LATE

Dear Ms. Fair:

Our installment note payment of $178.01 (Account #788G980) will be late this month because of a mixup with our bookkeeper. Please be assured that you will receive the payment in full no later than June 10.

Sincerely,

Alternative Phrase:

- After this, my payments will continue to arrive on time.

TO CREDITOR REPLACING NSF CHECK—BANK ERROR

Dear Ms. Graham:

I'm sorry that our check was returned to you marked NSF. We discovered that the bank failed to give us proper credit for our last deposit. Ms. McInery, the manager there, has promised to send you a letter of apology.

Enclosed is a replacement check for the full amount.

Thank you for your understanding.

Sincerely,

Alternative Phrases:

- The bank failed to credit us with a deposit, which is why our check was returned to you unpaid.
- The enclosed check will clear with no problems.

TO CREDITOR REPLACING NSF CHECK—OUR ERROR

Dear Ms. Kraemer:

There's really no excuse—our check to you bounced because we credited a large deposit twice. As you can imagine, we've had quite a time getting this problem straightened out. Enclosed is a cashier's check to replace the funds.

Thank you for your patience.

Yours truly,

Alternative Phrases:

- We're sorry our check to you was returned unpaid—we had credited a large deposit twice.
- The enclosed check should clear with no problem.
- We appreciate your understanding.

CORRECTING BILLING AND BANKING ERRORS

TO TELEPHONE COMPANY REGARDING A BILLING ERROR, ENCLOSING COPY OF CANCELED CHECK

Dear Ms. Gibbs;

As was discussed during our phone conversation today, I am enclosing a copy of both sides of my canceled check reflecting a payment of $278.77, which is the amount your most recent bill shows as past due.

My customer service number is 072116016. I would appreciate a new bill reflecting this credit.

Sincerely,

Alternative Phrases:

- Enclosed is a copy of both sides of my . . .
- Please send me a new bill reflecting this payment.

TO ELECTRIC COMPANY ASKING ABOUT A POTENTIAL BILLING ERROR

Dear Customer Service:

Our most recent bill, dated May 26, reflects a 50 percent increase over our previous bill. We feel this increase is highly unlikely; we haven't added any electrical equipment, nor has there been any marked change in the weather that might account for such an increase.

In fact, the only thing that has happened recently is the arrival of new tenants in Suite 26—the one next door to us. Is it possible that their power is going through our meter?

Enclosed is a copy of our bill and a check for $325.00, which reflects what we think is a more accurate amount. Please begin whatever procedure is required to monitor our exact usage. However, if it turns out that we are wrong, we will of course pay the difference at once.

Sincerely,

Alternative Phrases:

- We are concerned about the sudden increase—over 50 percent—in our bill.
- We will pay the difference at once if your monitoring shows this bill is accurate.

TO CREDIT CARD COMPANY REGARDING IMPROPER CREDIT FOR A RETURNED ITEM

Dear Mr. Heald:

Looking over our credit card statement from you this month, I find an error. On March 23, Steve Johnson used the card to purchase $115.97 worth of common brick. The following day, Steve returned the brick and received a credit chit. I've enclosed a copy of the chit so that you can track the charge and credit.

Thanks so much for working this out. We certainly are glad to be doing business with you.

Sincerely,

Alternative Phrases:

- There's an error in this month's statement from you.
- . . . and received a credit memo.
- I'd appreciate a new statement reflecting the credit.

TO BANK REGARDING A CHECKING ACCOUNT DEPOSIT ERROR—IN OUR FAVOR

Dear Mr. Wilder:

Much to my amazement, I've discovered our account, 371-987-89, has been credited with a deposit of $1,000.00 that we never made. Enclosed are copies of our deposit receipts for the last 60 days. I've also checked with Mr. John Blick, the other signer on the account, and he's made no deposits.

Can you straighten this out? We'd love to have the extra money, but I suspect someone else is already missing it.

Sincerely,

Alternative Phrases:

- Our statement, issued by you on April 25, credits us with a $1,000.00 deposit we never made.
- Please issue another statement showing that this deposit is no longer credited to our account.

TO BANK REGARDING A CHECKING ACCOUNT DEPOSIT ERROR—NOT CREDITED

Dear Mr. Morrison:

Thank you for your help on the phone today. Enclosed is a copy of both sides of our deposit receipt of April 4, showing a deposit of $5,432.10. Our account name and number appear on the receipt.

We would appreciate confirmation, with a phone call, as soon as this deposit has been properly credited.

Sincerely,

Alternative Phrases:

- As you requested, enclosed is a copy of both sides of our dated deposit receipt showing a deposit of $ . . .
- Please confirm in writing that this deposit has been credited to our account.

TO BANK REGARDING AN ERROR IN A LOAN PAYMENT

Dear Ms. Pierce:

Perhaps you can help. Your record of our payments on loan #17876 shows we have missed a payment; our records, however, show we have not. Enclosed are copies of all the canceled checks (eighteen in number) and copies of the receipts your office has sent to us when you received the checks. As you can see, not only is the number of payments correct, but the total dollar amount is also correct.

Please give me a call when you have this straightened out.

Sincerely,

Alternative Phrases:

- According to our records, we have not missed a payment on your loan #17876.
- I'd like confirmation in writing that we have been credited with the proper amount.

TO DEPARTMENT STORE REGARDING A BILLING ERROR

Dear Sir/Madam:

Our most recent billing (copy enclosed) does not reflect last month's payment. Although it's possible you received our check for $78.98 (copy also enclosed) after the bill was prepared, it seems unlikely because of the dates.

No matter how it happened, we'd appreciate a new bill reflecting proper credit.

Sincerely,

Alternative Phrases:

- Last month's payment is not reflected on this month's statement. I've enclosed a copy for your informatioh.
- Please send a new statement that includes last month's payment as a credit.

TO COLLECTION AGENCY THAT HAS MADE A MISTAKE

Dear Ms. Radson:

Your records show we still owe Waldo Point Harbor $750.00 for rent on Berth 27, Dock C, due December, 1986 and January, 1987.

Enclosed is a copy of a receipt from Waldo Point Harbor, signed by their secretary, dated March 13, 1987, showing payment of both the back due rental and the late charges. Also enclosed is a copy of both sides of the check we used to make the payment.

Please make the corrections on your record and send me a copy of the correction.

Sincerely,

Alternative Phrases:

- Apparently, you're still showing that we owe Waldo Point Harbor $750.00 back rent.
- I would appreciate a copy of the corrected record.

TO COLLECTION AGENCY SETTING UP A PAYMENT SCHEDULE

Dear Ms. Radson:

This will confirm our phone conversation concerning setting up a payment schedule for the $1,500.00 we owe Intelligent Solutions for computer equipment.

Enclosed is our check for $500.00; we will pay $500.00 on September 15, and $500.00, plus late charges of $75.00, on October 15.

Sincerely,

Alternative Phrases:

- Thank you for your help in setting up a payment schedule for the . . .
- The enclosed $500.00 is our first payment. We will send another $500.00 on the fifteenth of September and a final payment of $500.00, plus $75.00 late fees, on the fifteenth of October.

TO CREDIT AGENCY ASKING FOR ACCOUNT INFORMATION

Dear Ms. Radson:

We have recently been denied credit by Bridgeway Office Supplies, apparently because of information you're showing about our firm. We believe this information is in error.

Enclosed is our check for $10.00 as payment for a full printout of the credit information your agency has about our firm.

Sincerely,

Alternative Phrases:

- Apparently your firm has some incorrect information about our firm.
- We would like a copy of all the credit information you have about our firm. Enclosed is our check for $10.00 to cover the costs.

TO CREDIT AGENCY CORRECTING INFORMATION FOR A CUSTOMER

Dear Ms. Radson:

Mr. Paul Adelson of 325 Fourth Street in San Rafael asked us to confirm that he has paid us in full. We received his check for $375.00 on April 30. Please make the appropriate notation on your record.

Please call if you have any questions.

Sincerely,

Alternative Phrases:

- We'd like to help you update your records about Mr. Paul Adelson of 325 Fourth Street in San Rafael.
- He made payment in full to us with a check of $375.00 on April 15.
- If you need any more information concerning this matter, please get in touch.

TO CREDIT AGENCY CORRECTING INFORMATION FOR A BUSINESS

Dear Ms. Radson:

The End User's Center of Mill Valley has asked us to confirm that they have paid us in full. Although they were behind for several months, the new owners have been most cooperative about getting their account straightened out. Based on their performance, we have extended net-30-day terms to them again.

Please note the appropriate change in your records.

Sincerely.

Alternative Phrases:

- This letter will confirm that the End User's Center of Mill Valley have paid us in full.
- Since the store has new owners who have brought the account current, we have extended net-30-day terms to them.
- Perhaps you can add this letter to their file.

LETTER CONCERNING CONFUSION OVER INVOICES

Dear Ms. Abrams:

Today we received a second invoice, your #7560, for the telephone answering machines we purchased and paid for in July. Our records show we made payment in full with our check #2908 dated July 30.

If you need additional information, please give me a call.

Sincerely,

Alternative Phrases:

- The invoice, #7560, we received today shows we owe you for the telephone answering machines we purchased with check #2908 in July.
- Enclosed is a copy of both sides of the canceled check.
- Please send us a statement reflecting this credit.

LETTER ENCLOSING CANCELED CHECK

Dear Mr. Abrams:

Enclosed is a copy of both sides of our canceled check showing our payment in full for 200 reams of copier paper. As you can see, your endorsement is on the back of the check.

I trust this will straighten out the confusion. If you have additional questions, please give me a call.

Sincerely,

Alternative Phrases:

- The enclosed copy of our canceled check, with your endorsement, shows payment in full for the copier paper purchased in July.
- Please update your records to reflect this credit.

LETTERS ABOUT CREDIT

THANKS FOR YOUR INTEREST—ENCLOSING A CREDIT APPLICATION

Dear Mr. and Mrs. Sindicich:

Thank you so much for your decision to establish credit with us. Enclosed is the application form; you'll find that it's simple to fill out.

We will process your application as soon as we receive the completed form. As soon as your credit is approved, you'll receive two credit cards, a letter explaining your credit limits and other information, and a coupon for a special gift. Assuming everything is in order, you should receive your cards in about two weeks.

Sincerely,

Alternative Phrases:

- We are pleased you've decided to apply for credit with us.
- The enclosed application form is self-explanatory.
- Assuming your application is approved, you will receive two credit cards, a letter . . .
- You can look for your cards in about two weeks.

CHECKING A CREDIT REFERENCE

Dear Ms. Gray:

Susan and Dick Sindicich of 437 Pine Hill Road, Fairfax, have given us your name as a credit reference. If you'd take a moment to fill out the enclosed form and return it to us, we'd certainly appreciate it.

Sincerely,

Alternative Phrases:

- We would appreciate it if you would fill out the enclosed form and return it to us.
- . . . and return it to us within the next five days.

ACCEPTING CUSTOMER'S CREDIT AND OUTLINING TERMS

Dear Mr. and Mrs. Sindicich:

Your application for credit has been processed and approved. Enclosed are two credit cards; please be sure to sign them right away. Also enclosed is a brochure that outlines the details of our credit plan.

Your credit limit has been set at $500.00. If, after six months of prompt payment, you wish to increase your limit, please let me know.

Each month you will receive a statement of your account showing the amount charged, the amount paid, the minimum amount due, and the total amount due.

Please note that we charge no interest on payments made within 30 days of the initial billing; after that, the interest rate (APR) is 18 percent.

If you have any questions, now or in the future, please give me a call.

Sincerely,

Alternative Phrases:

- Congratulations! We are pleased to issue you two credit cards which are enclosed. Sign the backs immediately.
- We have established an initial credit limit of $500.00. This may be increased after six months of prompt payment.
- As a matter of policy, we charge no interest on payments made within 30 days . . .
- Write me if you have any questions. Be sure to include your credit card number in any correspondence.

REFUSING CUSTOMER'S CREDIT

Dear Ms. Lewis:

We are sorry to tell you that we cannot extend credit to you at this time because of information we received from Marin County Credit. Enclosed is a copy of their report.

If you feel their report is in error, or if you would like additional information, please contact them at the address shown.

Sincerely,

Alternative Phrases:

- Because of information we received from Marin County Credit, we will be unable to extend you credit with our store at this time.
- Questions about the report should be directed to Marin County Credit, 345 Fourth Street, San Rafael, CA 94964.

PROVIDING A CREDIT REFERENCE—POSITIVE

Dear Ms. Doty:

We are pleased to let you know that Linda Wilder of 3256 Village Green in Fairfax has been a credit customer of ours for four years. Her payments have been prompt, and there has been absolutely no problem with her account.

Sincerely,

Alternative Phrases:

- Linda Wilder of 3256 Village Green in Fairfax established credit with us over four years ago.
- Her record of payments has been excellent.
- We have no hesitation in recommending her as a credit customer.

PROVIDING A CREDIT REFERENCE—NEGATIVE

Dear Ms. Doty:

We are sorry to inform you that we have been forced to recall the credit card we issued to Ron Oldenberg of 890 Blithedale. Although he was a good customer of ours for several years, six months ago his account became seriously delinquent; in fact, we've been forced to turn it over to a collection agency.

Sincerely,

Alternative Phrases:

- We were forced to recall the credit card of Ron Oldenberg, 890 Blithedale, Sausalito, several months ago.
- We cannot recommend Ron Oldenberg of 890 Blithedale, Sausalito, as a credit customer because of problems we've had collecting his account.

REQUESTING INFORMATION ABOUT CREDIT DENIAL

Dear Ms. Doty:

I was distressed to receive your letter today turning down our request for credit. I know the references provided by our firm were of accounts in good standing. Apparently you made the decision on some other basis.

I would appreciate it if you would explain the reason for your decision, since I think it may have been based on erroneous information.

I look forward to your reply.

Sincerely,

Alternative Phrases:

- I was amazed that you turned down our credit application.
- Since the accounts I listed on the form are in good standing, you must have made the decision on some other basis.
- Please explain exactly why you turned down our application.
- I would appreciate a prompt response.

EXPLAINING CHANGES IN HOW AN ACCOUNT WILL BE HANDLED

Dear Mr. and Mrs. Brande:

The increase in our volume of business means we are employing the services of a professional, computerized billing service. This means several things.

1. You will be receiving statements from a different address: 1704 S. Broadway, Long Beach, CA 90802
2. The statements will be mailed on the fifteenth of each month and due on the first of the following month. A self-addressed envelope will be included for your convenience.
3. Any problems or questions should be sent to the new billing address. You can reach them by phone at (213) 555-0090.

We feel sure this change will result in better service.

Sincerely,

Alternative Phrases:

- We are changing to a computerized billing service.
- We have decided to hire a professional, computerized billing service.
- We know you'll appreciate the new efficiency.

LETTERS ABOUT DONATIONS

ASKING FOR MORE INFORMATION BEFORE DONATING

Dear Mr. Sommers:

Yesterday, I received a call about your project of restoring the tall ship *Galilee.* While I'm favorably inclined, I'd like to know more about your specific plans and your own qualifications before I contribute.

Please send me what you have, or, if you'd like, give me a call and we'll talk directly.

Very truly yours,

Alternative Phrases:

- I recently received information about your restoration of the tall ship *Galilee.*
- I'd like more information about you and your project.
- I'd be happy to talk with you in person.

ENCLOSING DONATION TO A WORTHY CAUSE

Dear Sir/Madam:

We are happy to contribute $100.00 to your education fund and will look forward to seeing our name appear on the list of contributors.

Sincerely,

Alternative Phrases:

- Enclosed is our donation of $100.00 to your education fund. We look forward . . .
- Thank you for the opportunity to help you further education about animals. Enclosed is our check for $100.

- We would be pleased if our name were included on your contributors' list.

ENCLOSING A DONATION TO A WORTHY CAUSE—WITH A QUOTABLE STATEMENT

Dear Nick,

I'm delighted to discover you think I have enough community influence to be worthy of being quoted in public. As you know, I'm solidly behind your efforts to preserve the free anchorage in Richardson Bay. Attached is a short statement to that effect which you're welcome to use in any way you can. I'm also enclosing a check for $200 to help your cause.

Thanks so much for the opportunity.

Sincerely,

Alternative Phrases:

- If I have any influence in this community, you're welcome to use it with the enclosed quote.
- You can count on my solid support of your efforts . . .
- Good luck with your efforts.

REFUSING TO DONATE TO A WORTHY CAUSE

Dear Mr. Hansen:

Although we recognize your efforts at educating the public about the humane treatment of animals, we are not in a position to contribute at this time.

Sincerely,

Alternative Phrases:

- Thank you for the opportunity to contribute to your efforts regarding educating . . .
- This is not a good time for us to contribute.

POSTPONING A DONATION TO A WORTHY CAUSE

Dear Ms. Feinman:

We certainly appreciate your efforts, and we do plan to contribute. Unfortunately, though, our cash flow dictates we will have to make our donation sometime in the late spring rather than now.

Keep up the good work.

Sincerely,

Alternative Phrases:

- Although we are unable to contribute at this time, please be assured of our support for your cause.
- We will not be able to donate until late spring.

REMINDER OF PLEDGE

Dear Mr. Lewis:

We haven't received your pledge of $60.00 yet. May we take a moment of your time right now? You may either send us a check or fill out the enclosed form to use your credit card. Then, slip it into the enclosed postage paid envelope and we'll handle the rest.

Thanks so much.

Alternative Phrases:

- Please take a moment right now to send us your pledge.
- The enclosed, postage paid envelope, is included for your convenience.

SPECIAL FUNDRAISING

Dear Ms. Goldman:

The enclosed brochure outlines an opportunity for us to increase both our services and our influence—all for a small amount of money. Since you're one of our staunch supporters, we're asking you to make an additional one-time donation so that we can act.

You may send a check or use the enclosed form to put your donation on your credit card.

We're looking forward to your prompt response.

Sincerely,

Alternative Phrases:

- We have a critical and immediate need, as outlined in the enclosed brochure.
- We're certain you'd like to contribute now so that we can act.
- Thank you for your support.

Chapter 3

LETTERS CONCERNING ORDERS

LETTERS ABOUT ORDERS

Follow-up on Order Not Yet Received
Follow-up on Phone Call
Adjustment Following Partial Return of an Order
Acknowledging a Claim—We're Checking and Will Get Back to You
Acknowledging a Claim—We Were Wrong
Acknowledging a Claim—We Think We're Right
Tracing Lost Orders
Enclosing a Refund
Refund Will Be Sent Later
Offer to Replace
Offer to Substitute
Explanation of Why Complaint Isn't Valid
Referring a Complaint to Another Person
Thanks for Your Opinion—No Other Action

In the business world, orders fall into two general categories: (1) orders placed for goods and services and (2) orders filled for goods and services. Since both categories can dramatically affect the cash flow of your business, letters dealing with orders must be handled with great care. For example, goods and services ordered improperly can cost your company a great deal of money, both in actual cash expended and in time spent straightening out the mistake. Moreover, confusion concerning orders placed with your company can not only cost money and time, but can result in customer dissatisfaction and lost future business.

SECRETARY'S TIPS ON WRITING LETTERS ABOUT ORDERS

1. *Be sure you understand the purpose of the letter.* Are you placing an order for goods or services or only seeking information? Are you filling an order or only responding to a request for information? Although these purposes seem obvious at first glance, secretaries report that there is often confusion on these points.
2. *Get all the information you need before composing the letter.* When you initiate simple orders, you probably have all the information you need at your fingertips. However, complex orders for goods or services usually require input from at least one other person. The same may be true when filling an order. If you take the time to gather all the necessary information before you start the letter, you'll save yourself both time and frustration.
3. *Determine the tone of the letter.* Letters concerning orders usually need to be straightforward. A slightly different tone may be required, however, when you're dealing with a com-

plaint—either one that your firm is making or one it is trying to resolve.

4. *The first paragraph should contain the most important information.* If possible, state exactly what you're ordering or how you're filling an order up front. If the information is complex, the first paragraph should sum up the information so that the person reading the letter knows exactly what to expect.
5. *Make it clear what response, if any, is expected from the reader.* When you're ordering goods or services, the response you expect is delivery of the goods or services you order. However, there is often a time factor that needs to be spelled out along with your order. If it's your firm providing the goods or services, performance may be all that's needed. Sometimes, however, you'll want receipts or confirmations.
6. *Be concise and complete.* Conciseness and completeness are extremely important when dealing with orders. The person receiving your letter needs to know exactly what he or she is dealing with in order to get the message. If you can boil that information down to a few simple sentences or a list, the transaction is much more likely to be satisfactory for all concerned.

LETTERS ABOUT ORDERS

FOLLOW-UP ON ORDER NOT YET RECEIVED (SERIES OF TWO LETTERS)

1.

Dear Sir/Madam:

We placed a telephone order for your spelling checker, "Spell Plus" on May 25, and gave you a Visa credit card number as payment. Unfortunately, we have not yet received the program.

Please phone and let us know when to expect the program.

Sincerely,

Alternative Phrases:

- On May 25, we ordered "Spell Plus" by phone and gave . . .
- The program has not arrived.
- Please send the product at once.

2.

Dear Sir/Madam:

We still haven't received the program, "Spell Plus," which we ordered on May 25. Attached is a copy of our letter of inquiry dated June 20 and a copy of our Visa receipt, indicating that you received payment in full.

If we do not receive the program by July 1, we will be forced to cancel the order and report our experience to the Better Business Bureau.

Sincerely,

Alternative Phrases:

- Although we've already written one letter, we still haven't received our copy of "Spell Plus." The program was ordered on May 25. Enclosed is both a copy of our first letter and a copy of our Visa receipt, . . .
- We will have to cancel our order and find another spelling checker if we don't hear from you by July 1.

FOLLOW-UP ON PHONE CALL (SERIES OF TWO LETTERS)

1.

Dear Mr. Miller:

I am writing to follow up on our phone conversation this morning and confirm that we have not yet received our order for 20 copies of Frank Alper's *Universal Law.*

As I said on the phone, we've received six requests for the book since Mr. Alper spoke here, and we'd like to fill them.

Thanks so much for your help.

Sincerely,

Alternative Phrases:

- As we discussed on the phone today, we are still looking for the 20 copies of *Universal Law* by Alper that we ordered June 3.
- Ever since Mr. Alper spoke at the Chamber meeting, we've been getting requests for the book, and . . .
- We appreciate your prompt attention to this matter.

2.

Dear Mr. Miller:

We still haven't received the 20 copies of Frank Alper's *Universal Law* we ordered on June 3. If we haven't received the books by July 1, we'll be forced to cancel the order.

Sincerely,

Alternative Phrases:

- Although in our phone conversation of June 12 you promised to ship the 20 copies of *Universal Law* at once, we will haven't received them.
- We'd rather not do business with another distributor, but if we don't receive the books by July 1, we'll have no choice but to look elsewhere.

ADJUSTMENT FOLLOWING PARTIAL RETURN OF AN ORDER

Dear Ms. Walsh:

Thanks so much for your prompt return of three copies of *Mommy, I Hurt.* We are crediting you with $1.50 each, a total of $4.50. The adjustment will show on your next statement.

I'm sorry the book didn't do well for you.

Sincerely,

Alternative Phrases:

- Enclosed is a copy of your credit slip for the return of three copies of *Mommy, I Hurt.* As you can see, each book cost you $1.50, for a total of $4.50, which will be reflected on your next statement.
- Your next statement will reflect a $4.50 credit for the three copies of *Mommy, I Hurt* you returned to us.
- We appreciate your business.

ACKNOWLEDGING A CLAIM—WE'RE CHECKING AND WILL GET BACK TO YOU

Dear Ms. Walsh:

Just a quick note to let you know we're following through on your phone call concerning the six missing copies of Frank Alper's *Universal Law.* I should have an answer for you by the end of next week.

I'm sorry about the problem.

Sincerely,

Alternative Phrases:

- We still haven't found the missing copies of Alper's *Universal Law.* However, today I'm shipping a second carton with six copies. If the original shipment shows up, please return it to us collect.
- If we haven't found the books by the end of the week, I'll ship another carton of six.
- Thank you for your understanding.

ACKNOWLEDGING A CLAIM—WE WERE WRONG

Dear Ms. Walsh:

I'm so sorry for the confusion about Frank Alper's *Universal Law.* You're absolutely right—you placed the order, and although we sent you the invoice, we never shipped the books. I personally made sure the books went out to you today and have waived the shipping costs because of the confusion.

Thank you for your understanding.

Sincerely,

Alternative Phrases:

- We've found the problem, and we created it. We did send you an invoice for ten copies of *Universal Law* by Alper, but we didn't send the books.
- The books went out today, and, because of the confusion, we have not charged you for this shipping.
- Good luck selling the books.

ACKNOWLEDGING A CLAIM—WE THINK WE'RE RIGHT

Dear Mr. Cooke:

We have received your inquiry about your order for fifteen copies of Frank Alper's *Universal Law.* We did receive your order on December

11, and it was processed immediately. In short, you should have received the books. Is it possible you have them but for some reason they didn't get recorded?

Please, give me a call, collect, and let's see if we can straighten this out.

Sincerely,

Alternative Phrases:

- According to our records, we shipped the fifteen copies of Alper's *Universal Law* on December 13.
- We are tracing the shipment and expect an answer by Wednesday.
- Would you double check—you may have received the books.
- Call me if there's still a problem. If I don't hear from you, I'll assume the books were found.

TRACING LOST ORDERS

1.

Dear Sir/Madam:

On October 31, you picked up two packages for local, same-day delivery. One was addressed to Karen Faire, American Independent Bank, 605 Olive, Los Angeles, California 90020. However, the package was never received by Ms. Faire. Please begin your usual trace procedure and let us know as soon as possible exactly what happened.

Sincerely,

Alternative Phrases:

- One of the packages we shipped through you has never been received. It was addressed to: Karen Faire, American Independent Bank, 605 Olive, Los Angeles, California 90020. You picked it up for local, same-day delivery on October 31.
- We assume you will be able to trace the package. Please let me know what happens next.

2.

Dear Ms. Faire:

We're sorry for the problem with our shipment. We checked with our delivery people, Speedy Delivery Service, and they show the original package was received and signed for by J. Brinnelle. Do you have such a person in your organization? If you do, please check and see if that person received the order and simply didn't deliver it to you. If no one by that name exists at your location, please give me a call so we can check further.

Sincerely,

Alternative Phrases:

- According to our delivery service, your order was received by a J. Brinnelle at your office, so you should be able to locate the package. However, if that doesn't help you find your order, let me know.
- Your order was delivered to your address. The package was accepted by someone named "J. Brinnelle" on October 31. Since there were no instructions to allow acceptance only by you, we have fulfilled our obligation to deliver.
- We show that your order was delivered to your address and signed for by J. Brinnelle. The next time you order, if you'd like to make sure we deliver only to you, please make that clear so that we can avoid this confusion in the future.

ENCLOSING A REFUND

Dear Mr. Crowell:

Enclosed is our refund check for $25.95. We're sorry our information packet, *Running Your Own Business,* didn't live up to your expectations.

Trusting in your continued good will, we are enclosing our catalog in the hope that you will find other booklets you'd care to order.

Sincerely,

Alternative Phrases:

- As promised, we're refunding your $25.95 for *Running Your Own Business.* Enclosed you'll find a check for that amount, along with a catalog that lists our other publications.
- Although this booklet didn't suit your needs, we're certain some of our other publications will, so we are enclosing a catalog of our current titles. Each carries the same no-questions-asked, money-back guarantee.

REFUND WILL BE SENT LATER

Dear Ms. Wayley:

Thank you for returning the crystal selection. We're sorry it didn't meet with your approval. As promised, we will return your money in full, including your return shipping costs. A check will be issued by our accounting department and will be in the mail to you no later than February 25.

Sincerely,

Alternative Phrases:

- We received your return of the crystal selection and are truly sorry it didn't meet with your approval.
- Your refund, including shipping costs, will be sent by our accounting department within ten days.

OFFER TO REPLACE

Dear Mr. Tripp:

We're sorry your Crystal Candle Holder, item 187, arrived damaged. As you know, we will either replace it or refund your money in full. Simply fill out the enclosed, postage-paid card, indicating your preference, and your refund or a replacement will be on the way.

Sincerely,

Alternative Phrases:

- Thank you for letting us know the Crystal Candle Holder you ordered was damaged in shipping.
- Use the enclosed, postage-paid card to let us know whether you'd like a replacement or a refund.
- We are sending you a replacement this week and trust it will arrive intact.

OFFER TO SUBSTITUTE

Dear Mrs. Kaufman:

We've been overwhelmed by orders for our Crystal Duck and are sorry to tell you your order arrived after we had sold the last one. We won't be able to get more, so we are offering you the opportunity to receive our newest item, the Crystal Rabbit. Normally, we would offer this item at $10.95, a full $2.00 over what you sent for the Crystal Duck. As you can see from the enclosed photo, the Crystal Rabbit is larger and more detailed than the Crystal Duck.

Unless we receive the enclosed, postage-paid card by March 15 indicating you'd rather have your money back, we'll send the Crystal Rabbit, knowing you'll truly enjoy it.

Sincerely,

Alternative Phrases:

- We underestimated the popularity of the Crystal Duck and received your order after we'd sold the last one.
- Unfortunately, we've discovered we won't be able to purchase any more Crystal Ducks; we have, however, discovered the Crystal Rabbit.

- If you don't want the Crystal Rabbit, please return the enclosed postage-paid card within 10 days, and we'll send you a refund check. If you do nothing, you can expect the Crystal Rabbit to arrive in about 20 days.

EXPLANATION OF WHY COMPLAINT ISN'T VALID

Dear Mr. Adams:

I was sorry to hear you weren't happy with the special cleaning we did for you at your offices on December 22. However, I must refuse your request for a partial refund for the following reasons:

1. We were told we would be able to enter your offices by 5:00 P.M. on Thursday, December 22. However, the conference room, where most of the preparation was needed, was occupied until 7:30, giving us a very short time to prepare.
2. As a result of the delay in access to the conference room, we were forced to do our cleaning around the caterers, who were trying to get set up. This confusion made our job tougher than it might have been otherwise.
3. Finally, in spite of your assurance that we would be able to begin our cleanup by 11:00 P.M., your guests were present until almost 1:00 A.M.

In view of these items, I'm sure you'll agree that we are due payment in full, even if the cleaning wasn't quite up to snuff.

Sincerely,

Alternative Phrases:

- I'm not surprised you were unhappy with the special cleaning. But given the circumstances, I think it's surprising we got anything done at all. Among the problems were:
- Perhaps you are unaware of the problems we had:
- Because of these problems, and because we worked around them, I think it's fair to say we performed our job as best as we were able to under the circumstances. Therefore, I'm refusing your request for a partial credit.

REFERRING A COMPLAINT TO ANOTHER PERSON

Dear Ms. Maxwell:

I was so sorry to hear you were not treated well by one of our waitresses on the evening of November 17. I've referred your complaint to the night manager, and I'm sure he will take appropriate action.

Meanwhile, enclosed is a coupon for two free dinners. I hope you will continue to enjoy our restaurant.

Sincerely,

Alternative Phrases:

- Thank you for letting us know you were poorly treated by one of our staff on November 17. Without this feedback, it is impossible for us to improve our customer service.
- Since the problem occurred after 8:00 P.M., I've sent a copy of your letter to our night manager. I'll follow through and make sure he has taken steps to correct the situation.
- As a way to apologize for the poor service you received and to say "thank you" for your willingness to let us know about the problem, I'm enclosing a coupon for two free dinners. You may use them any time during the next 60 days.

THANKS FOR YOUR OPINION—NO OTHER ACTION

Dear Mr. Gonig:

Thank you so much for the time you took to express your opinion on our proposed development. We appreciate your concern.

Sincerely,

Alternative Phrases:

- We appreciate your concern about the impact of our proposed development and are glad you took the time to write us a letter about it. You can be assured we do value your opinion and will keep your letter on file.
- We're sorry you don't share our enthusiasm for our proposed development and thank you for your letter of concern.
- Although we don't agree with your concerns about the impact of our proposed development, we do appreciate your taking time to write us about it.

Chapter 4

LETTERS ABOUT MEETINGS

CORPORATE MEETINGS

Calling a Board Meeting
Calling a Special Board Meeting
Requesting a Special Board Meeting
Enclosing Minutes of Board Meeting
Enclosing Proposed By-law Change, Asking for Comments

GENERAL LETTERS ABOUT MEETINGS

Requesting a Meeting
Explaining Anticipated Absence from a Meeting
Summing up a Meeting
Changing a Meeting Location
Meeting Reminder
Enclosing an Agenda

CONFERENCE ARRANGEMENTS

Requesting Bids on Conference Arrangements
Confirming Conference Arrangements
Thank You for Your Help with Our Conference

Business often seems to run on meetings. And since meetings are so important, correspondence about meetings is also important. In addition, letters that do such things as give notice of meetings, transfer voting rights, and sum up proceedings may form an important legal record and should be treated with due care.

If your business is incorporated, you will probably have to generate letters dealing with the legal aspects of corporations. Since corporate law varies from state to state, the letters here should be considered as guides only. Often, though, you'll find specific information about corporate affairs, including appropriate forms for correspondence, in the official corporate book that comes with the stock certificates. If you're unsure of how to proceed, consult the firm's attorney.

SECRETARY'S TIPS ON WRITING LETTERS ABOUT MEETINGS

1. *Be sure you understand the purpose of the meeting.* Are you, or is someone else, requesting or calling a meeting? What is the specific purpose of the meeting? These questions must be answered before you compose your letter.
2. *Get all the information you need before composing the letter.* When sending information about a meeting, be sure you know the date, time, and location of the meeting, as well as its purpose.
3. *Determine the tone of the letter.* Like most correspondence, the tone of letters about meetings will be the same as for any business letter. The only exception may be formal notices of corporate meetings, which may require specific language to make them official. Double check if you're not sure.

4. *The first paragraph should contain the most important information.* Let the recipient of the letter know in the first paragraph what's happening. If the letter is for information purposes only, say so. On the other hand, if the reader is expected to attend the meeting, spell that out.
5. *Make it clear what response, if any, is expected from the reader.* If you need to know who is coming to a meeting and who is not, let the recipient know how to respond. If no response is required, make that clear as well.
6. *Be concise and complete.* Meetings have a reputation of being time wasters. You can help set the pace with a concise and complete letter. Be sure you say enough, but don't say more than you need to.

CORPORATE MEETINGS

CALLING A BOARD MEETING

Dear Mr. Deams:

The annual board meeting of Fallbrook Real Estate, Inc., will be held in the company offices on Wednesday, July 15, 1990 at 9:30 A.M.

We will be electing officers as well as conducting other general business of the corporation, so it's important that you come.

If, for any reason, you cannot attend, please fill out the enclosed proxy form and return it to the company offices no later than 5:00 P.M. on Tuesday, July 14, 1990.

Sincerely,

Alternative Phrases:

- This letter is official notification of the annual board meeting of Fallbrook Real Estate, Inc. The meeting will be held at the company offices on Wednesday, July 15, 1990 at 9:30 A.M..

- In addition to general business, the election of officers will take place. Your vote is important.
- Enclosed is a proxy form which you may fill out and return if you are unable to attend the meeting. It must be received in our offices by July 14, 1990 in order to qualify.

CALLING A SPECIAL BOARD MEETING

Dear Mr. Deams:

We have recently received notice of a significant increase in the cost of our lease. According to our by-laws, authorization of such an expenditure must come from the board. Therefore, we must hold a special board meeting.

The special board meeting is called for Tuesday, March 21, 1990 at 11:00 A.M. at the company offices.

Unless I hear otherwise, I will assume that you will attend.

Sincerely,

Alternative Phrases:

- We are forced to call a special board meeting because we have received notice of an increase in our rent. Our by-laws state that authorization for such expenditure must be made by the board.
- The special meeting will be held at the corporate offices at 11:00 A.M. on Tuesday, March 21.
- Please let me know if you will be unable to attend.

REQUESTING A SPECIAL BOARD MEETING

Dear Ms. Jensen:

It has come to my attention that the property adjoining our building is for sale at what appears to be a reasonable price. I'd like you to call a special board meeting to discuss the possibility of purchasing the property.

Enclosed is the purchase information from the broker. Please include this information with the special board meeting notices so that everyone will be prepared.

Sincerely,

Alternative Phrases:

- I've recently become aware that the property adjacent to our corporate offices is for sale. The price seems reasonable to me, and I think it would be worth a special board meeting to discuss the possibilities of acquiring the parcel.
- When you send out the notices for the meeting, please include copies of the enclosed information.
- The enclosed information, provided by the real estate broker, sums up the situation well. I think it would be appropriate to enclose a copy with each special meeting notice.

ENCLOSING MINUTES OF BOARD MEETING

Dear Mr. Ryan:

Enclosed are the minutes from the special board meeting held on May 17, 1991. They are for your information only and will need to be approved at our next board meeting.

Sincerely,

Alternative Phrases:

- The enclosed minutes of the special board meeting are in draft form only; they will have to be approved at the next board meeting. If, in the meantime, you spot anything I've left out, please let me know.
- They are for your information only at this point. If you could take a moment to double check them for me, I'd appreciate it, since I can correct any omissions before they come up for approval at the next board meeting.
- Please take a few minutes to go over them so that you can be prepared for any additions or corrections at the next board meeting.

ENCLOSING PROPOSED BY-LAW CHANGE, ASKING FOR COMMENTS

Dear Mr. Ryan:

Enclosed are the proposed changes to the by-laws. These will be discussed and voted on at our next meeting. In the meantime, Mr. Gray, chairman of the by-law committee, has asked for comments.

After you've had a chance to study the changes, please send your comments to me, and I'll pass them along to Mr. Gray.

Thank you for your prompt attention to this matter.

Sincerely,

Alternative Phrases:

- The enclosed proposed by-law changes were generated by the by-law committee. They will be discussed and voted on at our meeting at 11:00 A.M., Wednesday, June 8 in the second floor conference room.
- You may drop your comments off to me, and I'll pass them along; or, you may send them directly to Mr. Gray.
- Please spend a few moments going over this proposal—your input is invaluable.

GENERAL LETTERS ABOUT MEETINGS

REQUESTING A MEETING

Dear Mr. Painter:

The Chamber is about to redesign its hats that promote Fallbrook. We'd like to combine our efforts with yours and create something that might work as a joint fundraiser for us and for your picnic.

I have several tentative designs, prices, and profit estimates, and I would like to get together with you to discuss them.

Please give me a call and let me know what would be convenient.

Sincerely,

Alternative Phrases:

- We know you're going to need some money to fund the annual Old Timer's Picnic and wondered if you'd be interested in joining us in redoing the hats that promote Fallbrook.
- Enclosed is a price list of hats in various styles and quantities. If last year is any indication, we should be able to generate between $2.00 and $5.00 per hat. Let's get together and discuss this in detail.
- I can arrange to meet with you almost any time. You can set up an appointment with my secretary or give me a call at home.

EXPLAINING ANTICIPATED ABSENCE FROM A MEETING

Dear John,

I know you're expecting me at the planning meeting on Monday, but I've been called out of town. A close relative in Iowa is ill, and I will be needed there.

I'm sure you understand, and I know you can get along without me.

Sincerely,

Alternative Phrases:

- I'm sorry I won't be able to attend the planning meeting Monday evening. There's an illness in the family, and I will be out of town. I shouldn't be gone any more than ten days.

- In spite of my good intentions, I will be unable to attend Monday's planning session since I've been called out of town for a family emergency.
- Thanks for your understanding. I'll give you a call as soon as I get back.

SUMMING UP A MEETING

Dear Dan:

I'm sorry to hear about your cousin and wish both of you the best.

We certainly missed you at our planning session Monday, so I thought you'd appreciate a summary of the meeting. Briefly, the following was decided:

1. The date was officially set for August 14.
2. We confirmed we would use Live Oak Park.
3. We authorized the Chamber to go ahead with their plan for hats, agreeing to pick up $200.00 of the costs and share equally in the profits.
4. We confirmed Jim Wayman as the main speaker.

As you can see, we got a lot done.

Sincerely,

Alternative Phrases:

- Each member of the planning committee asked me to express our best wishes and concern for you and your cousin.
- Enclosed is a copy of the news release that we issued after the meeting Monday. I think it sums up what we accomplished.
- We hope you'll be able to join us at the next planning session, scheduled for June 2 at the usual place and time.

CHANGING A MEETING LOCATION

Dear Billy,

Our regularly scheduled meeting for the Old Timer's Picnic on Tuesday, June 2 will be held in Room 22 at Fallbrook High School instead of Room 54 because of the election.

Room 54 is just below Room 22. Simply take the flight of steps down, turn left, and you're almost there.

Looking forward to seeing you on the second.

Sincerely,

Alternative Phrases:

- Tuesday's election has forced us to change the location of the Old Timer's Picnic meeting. Instead of room 54, we'll be meeting in room 22.
- It turns out room 54—the usual location for the Old Timer's Picnic meeting—is a polling place. This means we'll have to meet in room 22 next Tuesday.
- Instead of staying on the parking lot level, take the stairs down and turn left. Room 22 is the third door on your right.
- See you there.

MEETING REMINDER

The regular meeting of the South Bay Development Group will be held June 27, 1990 at 3:00 P.M. at the law offices of Marie Winslow, P.C., 512 E. Windsor Blvd. The map below will help you arrive on time. If you have any questions, call either me, at (213) 555-2176, or Mr. Winslow's office at (213) 555-7856.

Alternative Phrases:

- The South Bay Development Group will have its regular meeting on June 27, 1990 at 3:00 P.M. The meeting will be held at the law offices of Marie Winslow, P.C. Directions are shown on the map below.
- Architects' reports will be reviewed at the regular meeting of the South Bay Development Group on . . .
- You may call me at (213) 555-2176 if you need any additional information.

ENCLOSING AN AGENDA

Dear Jane,

Enclosed is the agenda for the upcoming management committee set for 7:00 P.M. on July 11. As you can see, we've got a lot to cover, but most of the reports should be brief.

See you there,

Alternative Phrases:

- The monthly meeting for the management committee is set for Tuesday, July 11 at 7:00 P.M. A copy of the agenda is enclosed. If you can't attend, please make arrangements for an alternate.
- I look forward to seeing you there,

CONFERENCE ARRANGEMENTS

REQUESTING BIDS ON CONFERENCE ARRANGEMENTS

Dear Sir or Madam:

The Phoenix Self-Publishing Association is looking for a place to hold our annual conference. Interest is running high and we expect many more people than last year. Could you look over these requirements and give us a bid?

Sincerely,

Alternative Phrases:

- Our organization, the Phoenix Self-Publishing Association, is planning its annual conference. The first step is to find a location.
- Enclosed is a list of our requirements. Would you contact me with some price information?

CONFIRMING CONFERENCE ARRANGEMENTS

Dear Carolyn,

After lots of committee meetings, and, as you know, lots of phone calls to you, I wanted to get our understanding about the conference arrangements down on paper so that we're all talking about the same thing. Enclosed is the information. If you have any questions, please give me a call.

Sincerely,

Alternative Phrases:

- Enclosed is a summary of the arrangements as they stand now.
- We've had the final committee meeting, and the enclosed is the summary of the results.

- I think we've covered everything. Give me a call if you have any questions.

1. Conference dates: (insert appropriate dates).
2. Number of people expected to attend: (appropriate number).
3. The audience to be seated on padded, folding chairs set up theater style, with a central aisle, and an aisle on each side.
4. A podium for the speaker with a table behind.
5. A banquet-type meal for 150 chosen from the enclosed menu.
6. We've reserved two suites for your speakers and enclosed a special rate card you may copy and distribute to your guests.
7. In addition to our usual excellent security, we've arranged for a security officer to escort people to the parking area following your Friday evening conference. Please let us know Friday morning exactly what time we can expect you to break up.
8. Simply have your attendees show their conference ticket to the parking attendant. There will be no additional charge for parking.

THANK YOU FOR YOUR HELP WITH OUR CONFERENCE

Dear Mr. Johnson:

Last weekend we held *Technical Writing for Nonspecialists Seminar* in your Cordovan room. I wanted to thank you and your staff for your help and support. I don't know what training you give your people, but it certainly works. Ann Mecham, your concierge, was able to solve every problem we had. And your dining room staff went out of their way to make sure the service was impeccable, in spite of several truly difficult customers. In fact, everyone, from the doorman to the housekeeper, did an outstanding job. We're looking forward to scheduling another seminar with you soon.

Sincerely,

Alternative Phrases:

- On October 20 we held our *Technical Writing* . . .
- Without the help and consideration of your staff, the event wouldn't have turned out so well.
- Your staff made our conference even more of a success.
- You can be sure that when we return to Los Angeles, we'll have the seminar there again.

Chapter 5

LETTERS THAT PROMOTE BUSINESS

SALES LETTERS

Introducing the Company
Enclosing Brochure
Asking for an Appointment
Confirming an Appointment
Thanks Following an Appointment
Requesting an Introduction
Introducing Another Person
Cold Call Letters
Confirming a Telephone Order
Thanks for Your Order
Thanks for Your Order with Additional Offer
Advance Sale Announcement to Valued Customers
Invitation to a Grand Opening
Welcome New Customer and Mention New Product

PROMOTION LETTERS

Survey Preceding Trade Advertisement Placement
Introducing New Representative
Suggesting Ad Copy to Retailers
Enclosing Tear Sheets from Ads

Every letter you write is an important tool in promoting your firm, but letters designed specifically to promote the business can be particularly effective. Large fees are regularly paid to professional writers and public relations companies to design letters aimed at selling products and services and to put businesses favorably in the public eye.

With a little thought and care, you, too, can learn to write letters as well as the experts.

SECRETARY'S TIPS ON WRITING LETTERS THAT PROMOTE BUSINESS

1. *Be sure you understand the purpose of the letter.* There is an important difference between letters that promote the business in a general sense and letters designed to sell. Promotion letters are those that put the company in a good light, while sales letters aim at selling a specific product or service. Be sure you know which kind of letter you're writing.
2. *Get all the information you need before composing the letter.* Correct information is particularly important when writing a sales letter. You need to have specific information about what you're selling, how long the offer lasts, and the terms of the sale. Promotion letters also require accurate information, but it's usually of a more general nature.
3. *Determine the tone of the letter.* The tone of your sales or promotion letter will reflect the image your firm wants to project. For example, if you sell spreadsheets to accountants you may want to be more formal than if you are selling computer games to teenagers.
4. *The first paragraph should contain the most important information.* If your letter is designed to sell a product or service,

name the product or service in your first paragraph. The following paragraphs can then present the details. If your letter is designed to promote the firm, you'll usually have a specific reason for doing so, such as introducing a new representative or suggesting ad copy to your retailers. State the purpose of your letter right away.

5. *Make it clear what response, if any, is expected from the reader.* Make it clear what action, if any, the recipient of the letter needs to take. If it's a sales letter, perhaps an order must be placed right away to take advantage of a special offer, or perhaps you need confirmation of a sales appointment. Many promotion letters require no action from the reader, but are simply sent to convey information and to keep the company's name in front of prospective clients.
6. *Be concise and complete.* Be sure you give enough information to get the response you want, but be careful to keep your letter as short as possible. Although some sales letters seem designed to persuade the reader to buy, that only works if the recipient keeps reading. While some argue that length has no correlation to effectiveness, by and large, shorter letters are more apt to work except in special situations. The same rule of thumb applies to promotion letters.

SALES LETTERS

INTRODUCING THE COMPANY

Dear Mr. and Mrs. Salk:

At last you can get your windows cleaned at a reasonable cost! We specialize in doing windows, inside and out, upstairs and down. We do it right, and we do it for less.

Our representative will be calling on you in the next few days to introduce our company, give you a free gift, and tell you about our services.

In the meantime, if you'd like more information, please call.

Sincerely,

Alternative Phrases:

- We offer excellent window cleaning at affordable prices.
- We are proud of our work and we do it well. Because we're efficient, we keep our costs low, which means we can charge you less.
- Our representative will be in your neighborhood soon. Give us a call, and we'll make sure he stops by with a free gift and specific information about our services.

ENCLOSING BROCHURE

Dear Dr. Costello:

Thank you for your interest in our new medical building at Park and Cherry. Enclosed is a brochure that not only gives basic information, but also shows some typical office suite floor plans.

As you know, we can design exactly the facility you require. We have a long history of creating efficient working space for the professional community.

If I can be of service, please call.

Sincerely,

Alternative Phrases:

- We were delighted to receive your inquiry about our new professional building at Park and Cherry.
- The enclosed brochure details both standard floor plans and financial arrangements.
- We can, of course, help you design your suite so that your office reflects your needs.
- Also enclosed is a list of clients, indicating our long history of serving the professional community.

ASKING FOR AN APPOINTMENT

Dear Ms. Hawkins:

We have received your postcard indicating your interest in a new BMW. I'd like to set up a test drive for you on either September 17 or 18. I'm available in either the morning or afternoon both days. Please give my office a call to set up an exact time.

Sincerely,

Alternative Phrases:

- Thank you for your inquiry indicating your interest in BMWs.
- Only a test drive can truly demonstrate the outstanding qualities of the car.
- We can arrange a test drive for you during either the morning or afternoon of . . .
- Simply call my office to arrange the details.

CONFIRMING AN APPOINTMENT

Dear Ms. Hawkins:

This will confirm our appointment for you to test drive a new BMW on Tuesday, September 17 at 11:00 A.M. at our Long Beach Boulevard location.

I'm looking forward to helping you put the car through its paces.

Sincerely,

Alternative Phrases:

- Thank you for taking time to test drive a new BMW on . . .
- Simply come to our offices at our Long Beach Boulevard. location and give this card to the receptionist.
- Plan on enjoying putting a new BMW through its paces.

THANKS FOLLOWING AN APPOINTMENT

Dear Dick,

Thanks so much for the opportunity to show you the new BMWs yesterday. I enjoyed meeting you and watching you as you put the cars through their paces.

I'll get back to you by phone early next week to get your reaction.

Sincerely,

Alternative Phrases:

- I really enjoyed meeting you, showing you the new BMWs, and watching you put the cars through their paces yesterday.
- I'm glad you took the time to test drive our new BMWs yesterday. It was a pleasure to meet you and watch you drive the cars.
- I'll give you a call soon so that we can talk about your reaction and the possibility of putting you in your own BMW.

REQUESTING AN INTRODUCTION

Dear Mr. Miller:

I have been moved and impressed with Frank Garner's books, particularly his *Modern Accounting Systems.* I wonder if you'd consider introducing the two of us the next time he's in town.

I'm involved in teaching several classes at Fairfax Community College. Over the year, I probably talk to several hundred people, so meeting Mr. Garner might be beneficial to both of us.

Looking forward to your response.

Sincerely,

Alternative Phrases:

- Would it be possible for you to introduce me to Frank Garner?
- Since I talk with several hundred people each year through my classes at Fairfax Community College, meeting Mr. Alper might be beneficial to both of us.
- Thanking you in advance,

INTRODUCING ANOTHER PERSON

Dear Frank,

I received the enclosed request last week and decided to suggest you give Jeff a call. He not only teaches classes at the college, but has a small planning/consulting business as well. I think you might find him an interesting and valuable person.

But I'll leave the final decision to you. If you'd like to make arrangements for the three of us to get together when you're in Washington County next month, let me know.

Sincerely,

Alternative Phrases:

- You may want to give Mr. Jeff Edwards a call. He's asked for an introduction—I've enclosed a copy of his letter—and I think you'd find him interesting.
- It hadn't occurred to me, but you may want to give Jeff Edwards a call and get to know him.
- Of course, it's up to you if you want to follow through. I could also set up a lunch for the three of us when you're in Washington County next month.

COLD CALL LETTERS

1.

Dear Mr. and Mrs. Oxford,

Enclosed is a copy of your plot map showing your property at 4375 Larkspur Place; you may find it useful.

According to our records, you have owned your home for ten years. As you undoubtedly know, property values in your area have increased tremendously since you purchased your home. If you'd like information about selling your home or investment properties in the area, I'd be delighted to talk with you.

I'll give you a call next week to see if I can be of service.

Sincerely,

Alternative Phrases:

- The enclosed plot map outlines your property at 4375 Larkspur Place. I've found most home owners appreciate having a copy and hope you find it useful.
- Our records show you've owned the house for over ten years. You're probably aware that the value of homes in your area has increased tremendously in that time.
- I'd be happy to talk with you about selling your home or finding investment property.
- I'd like to be of service, and I'll call you next week.

2.

Dear Dr. Griswald:

How would you like a free demonstration of the scientific word processor that allows you to include complicated formulae and symbology in your text *without* cut-and-paste?

SciWriter is a full-featured word processor that allows you to do just that. It was developed at a leading university to meet the rigid requirements of academic papers. Many department heads and their secretaries consider it the finest scientific word processor on the market today.

If you'd like our free demonstration disk, simply fill out the enclosed postage-paid card and return it to us. We'll send you the demo package along with additional information.

I look forward to hearing from you.

Sincerely,

Alternative Phrases:

- It's now possible to include complicated formulae and symbology in your word-processed text without cut-and-paste. And we can demonstrate just how easy it is.
- SciWriter was developed at a leading university to be a full-featured word processor and take advantage of your computer's graphic capabilities to allow multi-level formulae and symbols within the text.
- It is considered by many to be the finest scientific word processor available.
- You may have a free demonstration disk by filling out and returning the enclosed postage-paid card. With the demo disk, you'll also receive all the information you need to order SciWriter.

3.

Dear Mr. Oberg:

For years, we've been delivering papers for local professionals. We have a reputation for discretion, speed, and economy. We'd like to deliver your important documents, too.

Enclosed is a brochure showing our delivery area and our fee structure. I'll give you a call next week to see how we can be of service.

Sincerely,

Alternative Phrases:

- Proper and timely delivery of important papers and documents is a daily challenge for many professionals.
- We are well known for our discretion, speed, and economy.
- Enclosed is a map of our delivery area and a list of our fees.
- I'll check with you soon to answer any questions you may have and see how we can be of service to you.

CONFIRMING A TELEPHONE ORDER

Dear Dr. Griswald:

Thanks for your telephone order of three copies of the scientific word processor, SciWriter. The packages will be sent this week by UPS.

If you have any questions or need additional information, please give me a call.

Sincerely,

Alternative Phrases:

- Your three copies of SciWriter, the world's best scientific word processor, are being sent to you today by UPS.
- Don't hesitate to call our technical support division at (415) 555-8556 if you need any assistance.
- We truly appreciate your business.

THANKS FOR YOUR ORDER

Dear Ms. Edwards:

Thanks so much for your prepaid order of two computer work stations. The stations are being sent UPS and come with complete instructions.

Sincerely,

Alternative Phrases:

- We appreciate your pre-paid order for two computer work stations. They are being sent to you via UPS; you will find complete instructions in the packages.
- We trust you will enjoy the two computer work stations we are sending you via UPS. Complete instructions are in the boxes, and you'll be pleased to discover how easy they are to assemble.
- We received your pre-paid order for two computer work stations today. They will be shipped via UPS this week. You'll find complete assembly instructions in each box. We appreciate your business.

THANKS FOR YOUR ORDER WITH ADDITIONAL OFFER

Dear Dr. Griswald:

Thanks so much for your additional orders of two packages of the scientific word processor, SciWriter. We're glad you like it well enough to order more.

We've finally found a spelling checker we think supports SciWriter completely. It's called MasterSpell and includes a library of commonly used scientific terms, in addition to a standard 50,000 word dictionary. It's easy to use and lets you make corrections as you go or when you're finished with a file.

MasterSpell usually costs $150.00, but for a limited time we're able to offer the program at only $75.00 each.

To order, simply fill out the enclosed, postage-paid card indicating the number of copies you'd like, your purchase order number, and other method of payment, and we'll send them out at once.

Thanks again for your order.

Sincerely,

Alternative Phrases:

- Two packages of SciWriter, the scientific word processor are on their way to you.
- At last we've found a good spelling checker that totally supports SciWriter.
- MasterSpell retails for $150.00, but, because we're able to purchase the program in large quantities, we're able to offer it to our SciWriter users for only $75.00.
- Use the enclosed postage-paid card to order copies of MasterSpell.

ADVANCE SALE ANNOUNCEMENT TO VALUED CUSTOMERS

TO: Our Most Valued Customers
FROM: Strawberry Creek and Cream
RE: A Very Special Sale

We're getting ready for spring, and that means spring cleaning. For you, it means a Very Special Sale—two days of unadvertised, lower prices on at least 50 percent of our stock. Discounts for this event range from 10% to 60% off our regular low prices.

Our Very Special Sale begins Monday, March 15 at 10:00 A.M. and ends Wednesday, March 17 at 9:00 P.M.

Come and take advantage of these special values.

Alternative Phrases:

- Dear Valued Customer,
- We're having a very special sale . . .
- It's almost spring, and we're in the process of spring cleaning.
- On Monday, Tuesday, and Wednesday, March 15–17, we're having an unadvertised sale. You can take advantage of lower prices on over half of our stock.
- Come early to get the best selection.

INVITATION TO A GRAND OPENING

Dear Minneapolis Resident:

You've heard the rumors . . . you've watched the redecorating . . . now you're invited to our Grand Opening on Tuesday, September 18 at 10:00 A.M. in our new location, 1750 Blithesdale in downtown Minneapolis.

Much of our stock will be specially priced for this event. Come browse and enjoy refreshments on us.

Alternative Phrases:

- We'd like to invite you to our Grand Opening on (appropriate day, date, and time) at our new location, . . .
- We'll serve refreshments all day as you browse through our specially priced merchandise.

WELCOME NEW CUSTOMER AND MENTION NEW PRODUCT

Dear Ms. Nickles:

Congratulations on becoming a Crystal Palace customer. We're delighted to add you to our mailing list and want to let you know about our special "get acquainted" offer.

We have a selection of tiny, hand-blown glass animals, and we're offering them at our cost, $5.00 each, to new customers. These delightful pieces normally cost 10–$15.00 each, depending on their size.

So simply bring this letter with you, and we'll show you these delightful collector's items.

Sincerely,

Alternative Phrases:

- Thank you for stopping by our store and registering for our mailing list. We want to let you know about our special "get acquainted" offer.
- We're proud to offer our new customers a selection of tiny, hand-blown glass animals. After this event, the animals will be offered at $10 and $15, depending on their size. But for a limited time, for new customers, the price will be our cost—$5 each.
- Come and inspect these lovely collector's items. Bring this letter with you to take advantage of the special price.

PROMOTION LETTERS

SURVEY PRECEDING TRADE ADVERTISEMENT PLACEMENT

Dear Ms. Pender:

Our records show you ordered your first catalog from us within the last six months. We are trying to determine exactly how our mail-order customers find us. Some hear about us from friends, others through various magazines and publications; one customer even discovered us because of a wrong address!

Would you take a moment to fill out the enclosed postage-paid card and return it to us? In return, once we receive your card, we'll send you a $5.00 gift certificate to be used with any future catalog order.

Sincerely,

Alternative Phrases:

- We'd like to know how our catalog customers find us.
- We're trying to make the best use of our advertising budget so that we can offer even better service to our mail-order customers. In order to

place our ads most effectively, we need to know just how our catalog customers found us.

- This information is so valuable, we've decided to give a $5.00 gift certificate to any mail-order customer who completes and returns the enclosed, postage-paid card.
- Thank you for helping us in our efforts to improve our service.

INTRODUCING NEW REPRESENTATIVE

Dear Mr. Shandy:

We are pleased to introduce Sheila Quimby who will be servicing your account. Ms. Quimby graduated *cum laude* from Indiana University with a major in Business Administration and has spent the last five years in financial planning. When she joined us six months ago, she of course went through our extensive training program. We are convinced she will do an excellent job for you.

Sincerely,

Alternative Phrases:

- We've changed the way we're servicing our accounts in order to provide more responsive service. Sheila Quimby will be taking over your area and, as a result, your account.
- In addition to her degree, Ms. Quimby has received our own extensive training course.

SUGGESTING AD COPY TO RETAILERS

Dear Joe:

As we approach the beginning of the school year, we have an opportunity to sell the STUDENT TEACHER to students and teachers alike. With this in mind, we have designed some ad copy you may want to use in your regular ad program.

Enclosed are three camera-ready ads designed for local newspapers. All that need be added is your store's name, address, phone number, and business hours. As you can see, this information can be placed in the box provided, or the box may be cut off and the copy inserted under or over other copy.

When the ads run, we'd appreciate receiving tear sheets showing not only the ad, but the name of the paper and the dates the ads ran.

Sincerely,

Alternative Phrases:

- The beginning of the school years offers us an opportunity to sell the STUDENT TEACHER to students and their teachers.
- We know from experience that ads aimed at schools can pay large dividends.
- The enclosed ads are camera ready. They are designed for newspapers, and the paper can add your store's name, address, and phone number in the box provided.
- We'd appreciate copies of any ads you run during this campaign along with the name of the paper and the dates the ad appeared.

ENCLOSING TEAR SHEETS FROM ADS

Dear Mary:

As you know, we've been running ads for the STUDENT TEACHER in the sports section of the *Bangor Daily News* for the last three weeks. Enclosed are copies of those ads. Feel free to make as many copies as you like for promotion purposes.

Sincerely,

Alternative Phrases:

- Enclosed are copies of the tear sheets we've been running in the *Bangor Daily News* for the last three weeks.

- As you requested, we're enclosing copies of the advertisements we've been running for the STUDENT TEACHER. The date and paper are indicated on the appropriate copy.

ANNOUNCING UPCOMING AD CAMPAIGN

Dear Joe:

Starting Sunday, March 23, we will be running ads for *Golfer's Choice* magazine in the sports section of *The Gazette.* This campaign will continue for four consecutive Sundays. In conjunction with this, we will also be running 30-second spots on KLAC following their sports updates at 4:00, 5:00 and 6:00 P.M., Monday through Friday of the same four weeks.

You may want to take advantage of this exposure with additional advertising of your own. Enclosed is the copy we expect to use in both the newspaper and on the radio. Feel free to use these any way you like.

Sincerely,

Alternative Phrases:

- We're launching a two-pronged advertising campaign for *Golfer's Choice* on Sunday, March 23. Ads will be appearing in the sports section of the *Gazette,* and 30-second spots will be heard on KLAC following their sports updates at 4:00, 5:00, and 6:00 P.M., Monday through Friday. The campaign will continue for four weeks.
- The ads and scripts we expect to use are enclosed.
- We know from experience that "back-up" advertising in local media works, and we suggest you make arrangements now. You may use the enclosed copy as is or draw from it to create your own ads.

TO CHAMBER OF COMMERCE ANNOUNCING A NEW SERVICE

Dear Ms. Perin:

We're pleased to let you know that we've added property management to our services. As you know, recent population growth has meant an increase in the number of rental units. As a result, owners of rental units are faced with some particular problems, and we've designed our management around these needs.

Included in our services are the following:

1. Tenant screening. After taking a detailed rental application, we follow through with credit and reference checks.
2. Cleaning services. When a tenant leaves, we provide quick, thorough cleaning and minor repairs, so the unit is available almost immediately.
3. Maintenance. We've gathered some of the best people in the area to handle every sort of maintenance problem quickly and carefully.
4. Advertising. A special advertising program has been developed, complete with its own telephone number, to assure each unit is given ample exposure to prospective renters.

You know that our reputation for servicing buyers and sellers of real property is excellent. We will maintain the same high standards in property management.

Sincerely,

Alternative Phrases:

- In response to the increase in our area's rental units, we've added property management to our services.
- We've worked hard to address the problems owners of income property have.
- We will bring our expertise in servicing clients to our new venture.

TO TRIM A MAILING LIST

Dear Friend:

Our mailing list has grown beyond manageable limits, and although we're happy to continue sending our newsletter to anyone who wants it, we need to be sure you do want it.

Enclosed is a postage-paid card. If you'd like to continue receiving our newsletter, simply check the box marked "Yes."

There's space for an address change, or any other comment you'd like to make.

If we don't receive your card by the end of the month, we'll be forced to remove your name from our mailing list.

Thank you for your help.

Alternative Phrases:

- It's time to trim our mailing list by eliminating the names of those people who no longer wish to receive our newsletter.
- To continue receiving our newsletter, simply fill out and return the enclosed postage-paid card.
- We'll remove your name from our mailing list if we don't hear from you by November 2.

REMOVE MY NAME FROM YOUR MAILING LIST

Dear Ms. Wallace:

Please remove my name from your mailing list. I'm not sure how I got on your list to begin with. I am not a physician and, thus, have very little interest in your products.

Sincerely,

Alternative Phrases:

- I'd like my name removed from your mailing list.
- Since I don't practice medicine, I don't know how my name appeared on your list in the first place.

REQUESTING ADVERTISING RATES

Dear Sir/Madam:

Our firm specializes in computer hardware and software for writers, and we believe your magazine might be an excellent place for us to advertise.

Please send us your current rate card for both display and classified ads. We'd also appreciate any demographic information you might have available.

Thank you,

Alternative Phrases:

- We're interested in advertising in your publication and would like a media kit to help us determine exactly what's involved.
- As specialists in computers for writers, we're looking for the right magazine to place our ads in.
- In order to make this decision, we need specific demographic information, as well as advertising rates.

PLACING AN AD IN A MAGAZINE

Dear Janice:

Enclosed is camera-ready copy for our advertisement to be run in the January, February, and March issues of *Profiles Magazine.* Also enclosed is our signed contract.

If you have any questions, please give me a call.

Sincerely,

Alternative Phrases:

- Enclosed is our signed contract and camera-ready art for an ad to run in your January, February, and March issues.
- I believe everything is in order. If not, please give me a call.

PUBLIC RELATIONS FIRM ASKING FOR A PROPOSAL

Dear Sir:

Our firm specializes in computer hardware and software for writers. We think that we could expand our business considerably by adding mail order, but we are not sure of how to go about this in the most effective and economical way.

We understand you've worked with computer companies and have experience in both public relations and advertising. We'd like to get a proposal from you.

We recognize that you will need a great deal more information than can be handled in a letter. However, we can probably get started with this letter and the enclosed copies of all our current promotion pieces. I hope they will help you understand our concept.

If you're interested in pursuing this with us, please give me a call to set up an appointment.

Sincerely,

Alternative Phrases:

- We know we could expand our hardware and software sales to writers by including mail order, but we need some help in planning the campaign and choosing media.
- Your reputation with computer companies is excellent, and we'd like to discuss the possibilities of working with you.
- The enclosed copies of our current ads will give you some idea of what we offer.

LETTER TO A COLUMNIST

Dear Columnist:

We understand you need to maintain your anonymity in order to write an objective column. But we wanted to let you know what we're doing.

Our restaurant, The Pizza Place, will open Monday, September 15. In addition to pizza, we will be serving a variety of authentic Italian dishes, including a daily lunch and dinner special. We've enclosed a copy of our menu to give you an idea, but you won't know what a good job we're doing until you try our food for yourself.

We'd offer you a complimentary meal, but recognize that isn't appropriate. In any event, we hope you'll give us a try and a review.

Sincerely,

Alternative Phrases:

- I've enjoyed your column over the years and wanted to let you know I've finally opened my own restaurant.
- Enclosed is a copy of the menu.
- Enclosed is a coupon we've sent to 500 local residents. You can use it and still remain anonymous.

CONFIRMING A TELEPHONE ORDER FOR A NEWSLETTER

Dear Jody:

Enclosed is the camera-ready copy for our newsletter. As I said on the phone this morning, we'd like 5,000, folded in thirds for mailing, printed on Eaton Ivory in Pantone 463U.

We'll look for your delivery Friday, and expect to be billed net 30 as usual.

Thanks so much for your help.

Sincerely,

Alternative Phrases:

- This will confirm our telephone order for 5,000 newsletters. We'd like them printed on Eaton Ivory using Pantone 463U, and folded in thirds for mailing. Camera-ready art is enclosed.
- Per our phone conversation:
  5,000 copies
  Eaton Ivory Stock
  Pantone 463U ink
  Folded in thirds for mailing
- Unless we hear otherwise, we'll expect delivery to our offices on Friday, November 29, with the usual net 30 billing.

CONFIRMING A TELEPHONE ORDER FOR DISPLAY ADVERTISING

Dear Sam:

This will confirm our telephone conversation this morning about running our ad again next week with the following changes:

1. A "SOLD" banner over the house priced $249,000.
2. The $375,000 price reduced to $350,000.
3. The hours of our office changed from "9:00 A.M. to 5:00 P.M." to "9:00 A.M. to 6:00 P.M."

Thanks for your help.

Sincerely,

Alternative Phrases:

- The following sums up our conversation about the changes needed in our ad:
- We've had good results with ads in your paper and appreciate your help.

CONFIRMING A TELEPHONE CONVERSATION ABOUT A MISTAKE IN ADVERTISING—ASKING FOR CREDIT

Dear Sam:

I'm sorry this has been so confusing! But as I said on the phone this morning, the price should have been reduced to $350,000 instead of the original $375,000.

This will confirm our credit of $25.00 for the error.

Thanks for your understanding.

Sincerely,

Alternative Phrases:

- Thank you for agreeing to a credit of $25.00 for the mistake your typesetter made on our ad. As I explained on the phone this morning . . .
- As you requested, this will confirm that the price in our ad should have been reduced to $350,000 instead of $375,000 as was printed.

ASKING FOR BIDS ON LOGO DESIGN

Dear Sir/Madam:

We feel our logo is old-fashioned, and we are considering a new design. In addition to our letterhead, I've enclosed a couple of other promotion pieces to give you a sense of our business.

Would you please let me know what you think a re-design would cost?

Sincerely,

Alternative Phrases:

- It's time to update our logo.
- We'd like to know how much it would cost to redesign our logo.

- Our logo, as shown on the enclosed stationery and promotional pieces, is due for a re-design.

ASKING SOMEONE TO MAKE A SPEECH

Dear Mr. Wayman:

The annual Hillsdale Realtors Annual Dinner is coming soon, and we'd like you to make the keynote address. We feel this is particularly appropriate, since this year marks the 50th Anniversary of your real estate office.

As I understand it, your father actually founded the firm. We'd love to hear some stories about him and about early development in the area.

The Dinner will be held at the Villa Amalfi on Sunday, October 7. Cocktails will be served beginning at 5:00 P.M., and the program is scheduled to start at 6:30. We'd like you to talk for about twenty minutes.

Please let me know as soon as possible one way or the other.

Sincerely,

Alternative Phrases:

- We'd like you to be our featured speaker at the annual Anniversary Dinner.
- This year's Annual Dinner coincides with the 50th anniversary of our real estate firm, and we'd like you to be our keynote speaker.
- I gather that, as a youngster, you helped your father establish the firm. Perhaps you could talk about him and some of the firm's early developments.
- Twenty minutes or so should be enough.

ACCEPTING A SPEAKING ENGAGEMENT

Dear Mary,

Thanks so much for your invitation to speak at the conference. I'd be delighted.

Keep me posted about the details.

Sincerely,

Alternative Phrases:

- Thank you so much for your kind invitation to speak at the conference. I am pleased to accept.
- I assume you'll inform me of the final schedule.

REFUSING A SPEAKING ENGAGEMENT

Dear Mary,

I'm sorry I'm going to have to refuse your kind invitation to speak at the Chamber luncheon. Unfortunately, I'm scheduled to be in Washington that week, and there's just no way to change my plans.

May I suggest you contact Vern Wilt? He too has been in the area a long time and can tell a good story in public.

Good luck, and thanks again.

Sincerely,

Alternative Phrases:

- I was pleased to receive your invitation to speak at the Chamber luncheon. To my sorrow, I'm forced to decline.

- Perhaps Vern Wilt would be willing to give a talk.
- Mr. Wilt has also been in the area a long time and is well known for his ability to speak in public.

BIRTHDAY LETTER TO A CUSTOMER

Dear Charlotte,

We wish you a happy birthday and want to thank you for being our customer with the enclosed gift certificate.

Many happy returns.

Sincerely,

Alternative Phrases:

- Congratulations on your birthday. We want to thank you for being a valued customer with the enclosed gift certificate.
- Please accept both our congratulations and enclosed gift certificate in honor of your upcoming birthday. We truly appreciate your business.

Chapter 6

NEWS RELEASES AND NEW PRODUCT RELEASES

One of the best ways to get free publicity is through news releases and new product releases. Newspapers and magazines are hungry for information and welcome properly prepared information they can use. This is particularly true for local papers and trade magazines which often have a small staff and a well targeted audience.

Almost any business event has the potential of some free press through a news release: a new employee, a new service or product, a move, the addition of space, the participation of an employee in a civic event, marriages, births, graduations, etc. It's mostly a matter of recognizing that the event has potential news value and submitting the proper form of news release.

New product releases are equally important sources of news. Any time your company releases a new product—new to your company, not necessarily new to the world—there's an opportunity to spread the word through local and trade publications.

SECRETARY'S TIPS ON WRITING NEWS RELEASES AND NEW PRODUCT RELEASES

1. *Be sure you understand the purpose of the release.* The purpose of all news and product releases is, of course, to get some publicity for your firm. But there can be more to it than that. When you're dealing with a product release, the product is the important information; a news release may feature the company, information about the company, or an individual within the company.
2. *Get all the information you need before composing the release.* This can be particularly important with product releases to technical trade magazines. If you're using technical specifications, be sure they're accurate and complete.

3. *Determine the tone of the letter.* Most releases are businesslike in tone. Determining the exact tone is really a matter of understanding your audience. If it's a technical audience, your language will be a bit different than if it's a general audience.
4. *The first paragraph should contain the lead.* A lead contains the "hook"—the information that will get the reader to read the rest of the story. It should contain the basic information, like "new hours" or "new software," the name of the firm, and a phrase like, "it was announced today."

   The second paragraph should contain the details, and should attribute the story to someone—usually the owners or an officer of the firm.

   The paragraphs that follow might contain a quote, background information, or both. Keep in mind, however, that some of your information may be cut by the publication in the interest of space and conciseness.
5. *Make it clear what response, if any, is expected from the reader.* When you're releasing product information be sure to include ordering information, including price. In more general news releases, you won't be looking for a specific response, but you'll want to make sure the reader knows how to find your firm.
6. *Be concise and complete.* A simple, concise style is best. Be as complete as necessary, keeping in mind that some of your information may not appear in print. Keep your release to a single page if possible.

NEWS RELEASES

News offices are busy places, and reporters need to have the basic information within easy reach. The following form, used on your letterhead, will give your release a professional look and help orient the reporter quickly:

DATE:	This is the date the release is sent out.
RELEASE DATE:	This is earliest date you want the information printed. You may replace this date with "For Immediate Release," if that's appropriate.
SUBJECT:	Use a brief phrase here, such as "New Hours at Homestead Realty" or "Peregrine-Falcon Announces New Software."
CONTACT:	Provide name and phone number of the person the newspaper should contact to ask questions and confirm information.

The above information is followed by the text of your release. It should be typed in upper and lower case, just like a letter, but it should be double-spaced so that the editor can easily make corrections.

At the end of your news release, type END or type three number signs (###) in the center of the page. This lets the reporter know he or she has all the material. (Don't use the old-fashioned "30"—this will mark you as an amateur.)

ANNOUNCING NEW HOURS

FOR IMMEDIATE RELEASE

SUBJECT: NEW HOURS AT B & J FLOWERS
CONTACT: Bonnie Beemer, 555-3784

Buying flowers for loved ones and special occasions is easier this spring because B & J Flowers has extended its hours, it was announced today.

The flower shop, located at 243 South Main, is now open until 6:30 P.M., Monday through Saturday, according to owners Bonnie and Jack Beemer. The store will continue to open daily at 9:00 A.M. and will close at 4:00 P.M. on Sunday.

"We have so many lovely flowers this spring, Ms. Beemer said, "We wanted to make them more available to everyone."

The store, which has been in the same location since 1953, gets as many flowers as possible from local sources, it was reported.

The Beemers have studied flower arranging and enjoy creating special floral effects.

Alternative Leads:

- Celebrating love and special occasions with flowers is easier . . .
- Additional hours make it easier to buy flowers at B & J Flowers, it was announced today.

ANNOUNCING A NEW EMPLOYEE

FOR IMMEDIATE RELEASE

SUBJECT: Janet Seidler is new technical support specialist.
CONTACT: Lewis Todd, 555-6732

A new technical support specialist has been brought on board at Peregrine Falcon Co., it was announced today.

Peregrine Falcon Co. distributes the popular spreadsheet program, Compaccount. "Providing technical support for our users is important to us," President Robbin Klaus said today.

Janet Seidler replaces David Addelson who, although still associated with the firm, has returned to graduate school. Ms. Seidler comes to the area from Columbus, Ohio, where she worked at Ohio State University. In addition, she is a co-author of two computer books and has served on the editorial staff of two computer magazines.

"Compaccount is an amazing program," she said. "It provides a lot of flexibility. It's easy to use; but because it does so much, users often have questions in the beginning."

Alternative Leads:

- Getting technical support will be even easier with the addition of a new tech-support specialist, Peregrine Falcon Co. announced today.
- The technical support division of Peregrine Falcon Co. has brought on a new specialist it was announced today.

ANNOUNCING A NEW SERVICE

RELEASE ON: September 9, 1991
SUBJECT: House Cleaning Service Opens
CONTACT: Kim Ehrlich, 555-3434

A single phone number will find you a competent, bonded house cleaner according to Kim Ehrlich, founder and owner of "Clean Sweep," the town's first cleaning service.

"We have a staff of fully trained and fully equipped men and women who will come clean your house," Ms. Ehrlich said today. Each staff member has been personally trained by Kim who has been cleaning houses professionally for over 15 years.

"Clean Sweep" can be reached by calling 555-3434 during business hours.

Alternative Leads:

- A competent, bonded house cleaner can be found with a single phone call according to Kim Ehrlich . . .
- One phone number will get you competent, bonded help with house cleaning according to Kim Ehrlich.

ANNOUNCING A NEW PRODUCT

FOR IMMEDIATE RELEASE

SUBJECT: Thesaurus for RITEWELL
CONTACT: Al Wiley, 555-2255

It's now possible to find more accurate and appropriate word choices on documents generated by the popular word processor, RITEWELL, it was announced today.

Super Software, the locally owned distributor of RITEWELL, began taking orders for their new product, Word Finder, this week. "The response has been good," said Jim Dooty, chairman of the board. "Even professional writers have trouble finding just the right word it seems, and Word Finder allows them to find that appropriate word in a matter of seconds.

The new product, which will run on any computer system that runs RITEWELL is offered for $75.00. For additional information, contact: Super Software, 123 State Street, Newton, New York 14235.

###

Alternative Leads:

- Finding that exact word you want in your documents is now easier, distributors of the RITEWELL word processor announced today.
- Improving professional papers on computers is now a breeze according to Super Software, distributors of the popular word processor, RITEWELL.

ASKING FOR A CORRECTION TO A NEWS STORY

Dear Ms. Hunsaker:

Thank you for your story about our new thesaurus program, Word Finder, in Friday's paper. We appreciate the publicity.

However, somehow the price was wrong. The price for Word Finder is $55.00, not $75.00 as reported.

We'd appreciate a correction as soon as possible.

Sincerely,

NEW PRODUCT RELEASES

Most new product releases are sent to magazines, which are just as busy as newspapers. New product releases should follow the same general form as news releases, but with one important addition.

When possible, a black and white photo of the product should be enclosed with the release. If you do enclose a photo, so indicate in the heading. Sometimes, the magazine will take the picture if you enclose the product or the box the product comes in. If neither is possible, just write the release.

The following form, used on your letterhead, will give your release a professional look and help orient the magazine staff quickly:

DATE:	This is the date the release is sent out.
RELEASE DATE:	This is the earliest date you want the information printed. You may replace this date with "For Immediate Release," if appropriate.
SUBJECT:	Use a brief phrase here, such as "New Line of Preserves from Homestead Canning" or "Blue Heron Enterprises Announces New Software."
CONTACT:	The name and phone number of the person the newspaper should contact to ask questions and confirm information.
	BLACK AND WHITE PHOTO ENCLOSED

The above information is followed by the text of your release.

At the end of your news release type END or type three number signs (###) in the center of the page. This lets the reporter know he or she has all the material.

ANNOUNCEMENT WITH A PICTURE ENCLOSED

FOR IMMEDIATE RELEASE

SUBJECT: Keytops Now Available for LingoWrite
CONTACT: Bonnie Beemer, 555–3784

BLACK AND WHITE PHOTO ENCLOSED

Keytops showing users which function keys produce which symbols are now available for the multi-language word processor, LingoWrite, it was announced today.

According to technical support specialist, Stuart Goldman, the keytops will make it easier for users to remember and use all the available symbols. "The tops are actually plastic sleeves designed to slip over the function keys on IBM and IBM-type keyboards. Each top carries the symbol and the original function key number so that it can be left in place permanently," he said.

A set of ten keytops costs $29.95 and can be ordered direct from Blue Heron Enterprises, 50 W. High Street, Clark, Indiana 47123.

###

Alternative Leads:

- Users of the multi-language word processor, LingoWrite can now add keytops showing the symbols for their function keys, it was announced today.
- Locating symbols is easy now with the new keytops for the multilanguage word processor, LingoWrite.

ANNOUNCEMENT WITH A SAMPLE ENCLOSED

FOR IMMEDIATE RELEASE

SUBJECT: Portable Hot Stuff Taco Sauce by Pepper & Co.
CONTACT: Betty Guest, 555-7277

SAMPLE ENCLOSED

Hot Stuff, the locally produced taco sauce, is now available in a small plastic pouch, ideal for picnics and other away-from-home uses, it was announced today.

"So many people want to put our sauce on almost anything they eat, but they didn't want to carry the bottle with them," owner and developer Betty Guest said. "The plastic pouch makes our Hot Stuff truly portable."

The plastic pouches will be available in boxes containing 24 servings and sold in most grocery stores.

###

Alternative Leads:

- People eating away from home will be able to enjoy locally produced Hot Stuff taco sauce in a new plastic pouch, it was announced today.
- A small, plastic pouch makes it easy for people to enjoy locally produced Hot Stuff taco sauce away from home, it was announced today.

Chapter 7

LETTERS OF THANKS AND CONGRATULATIONS

LETTERS OF THANKS

For Information
For the Public Compliment
For the Suggestion
For the Referral
For the Gift
For the Interview
For Your Time
For Your Help
For Your Support (series of 2)
Thanks for a Product
Thanks for the Introduction

LETTERS OF CONGRATULATIONS

On Your Engagement
On a Marriage
On a Birth
On a Graduation
On a Civic Award
On a Speech
For Mention in a Publication

On an Anniversary
On a Scholarship
On a New Home
On Your Retirement
On an Employment Anniversary
On a Promotion
For Election to Service Club Office

Letters of thanks and congratulations are good business. Acknowledging a job well done is always worth doing; it not only makes the person in question feel good, but it encourages excellence. The same thing is true about offering congratulations.

The business that takes time to send thank you and congratulations letters is not only spreading goodwill, it's also demonstrating that it's aware and interested in its community. Although it's probably impossible to track direct quantifiable results from such letters, it's a practice well worth doing.

Letters of thanks and congratulations need not be complex or take a lot of time. In many situations, cards can be used, which make the process even easier and more efficient. Many secretaries report that they keep a selection of birthday, thank you, congratulations, and other cards handy for such occasions. Others say they maintain a small stock of blank cards so that they can quickly write a note by hand. Actual letters, of course, can be used in any situation and may offer a more personal touch.

SECRETARY'S TIPS ON WRITING LETTERS OF THANKS AND CONGRATULATIONS

1. *Be sure you understand the purpose of the letter.* Most letters of this nature are quite straightforward, so their purpose is fairly obvious. Just be sure you're clear about the purpose so you don't congratulate someone on an anniversary when you mean to wish them happy birthday.
2. *Get all the information you need before composing the letter.* When sending letters of thanks or congratulations, it's nice to have all the facts. Accurate numbers, dates, degrees, and so on add a personal touch.

3. *Determine the tone of the letter.* Most letters of thanks and congratulations can be informal in tone. Once in a while, as in the case of congratulating a relative stranger on receiving an advanced degree, or a politician on election, you may want to be more formal.
4. *The first paragraph should contain the most important information.* State up front your reason for thanks or congratulations. Sometimes, a simple first paragraph will be enough; at other times you may want to go into more detail.

LETTERS OF THANKS

FOR INFORMATION

Dear Mary,

Thank you so much for the survey of Middletown businesses. The information not only came promptly, but proved to be extremely valuable for our planning session.

Sincerely,

Alternative Phrases:

- We certainly appreciate your prompt delivery of the survey of Middletown businesses. As we expected, the data are extremely useful to us.
- I wanted to take a moment to thank you for the information you sent us about businesses in Middletown.
- We recognize the effort you put in to be able to deliver the information so quickly.
- Our planning session was much easier because of the data you provided.

FOR THE PUBLIC COMPLIMENT

Dear Bill,

I was delighted at the compliment you gave me and my firm on your broadcast this morning. We've been working hard to make a difference in the community, and it's nice to know it's been noticed.

Thanks so much, and keep up the good work.

Sincerely,

Alternative Phrases:

- Thank you so much for your kind words about me during this morning's broadcast.
- I was delighted you mentioned our firm in such a positive way in your broadcast on October 10.
- Not only do we think our efforts are important, but we enjoy performing the service.
- It's nice to know our efforts are noticed and appreciated.

FOR THE SUGGESTION

Dear Ms. Jones:

We appreciate the time you took to suggest a specific plan for dealing with the homeless in our area. It's good to know people are truly interested and willing to think creatively.

Sincerely,

Alternative Phrases:

- Thank you for your suggestions about dealing with the homeless in our area. You can be sure we will consider your ideas.

- It was a pleasure to read your letter outlining your thoughts on solutions for our area's homeless problem. Thank you so much for the time you took to write us.
- I wanted to let you know we received your plan for dealing with our area's homeless. Thank you for your interest.

FOR THE REFERRAL

Dear Russ,

Thanks so much for referring Mr. and Mrs. Walker to me for legal services. They've become good clients, and we expect to continue to do business together.

Sincerely,

Alternative Phrases:

- Just a quick note to thank you for referring Mr. and Mrs. Walker to our offices.
- Mr. and Mrs. Walker contacted me today, and I wanted to thank you for the referral. You can be sure I will do likewise when the occasion arises.

FOR THE GIFT

Dear Marie,

The flowers you sent for our Grand Opening were lovely and added a truly classic touch. We received many compliments and were delighted to tell people where they could find you.

Thanks so much for your thoughtful gift.

Alternative Phrases:

- Thank you for the beautiful flowers you sent for our Grand Opening.
- Your gift of flowers for our Grand Opening was certainly appreciated.
- It was a pleasure to receive so many compliments and let people know how they could contact you.

FOR THE INTERVIEW

Dear Mr. Samuels:

Thank you for the interview yesterday. I appreciate both your time and your interest in me as a candidate for your sales position.

Enclosed are the additional references you requested.

I'm looking forward to hearing from you.

Sincerely,

Alternative Phrases:

- I certainly enjoyed our talk yesterday and wanted to thank you for both your time and . . .
- My interview with you yesterday was truly enjoyable. Thank you for your time . . .
- I will give your office a call next week if I don't hear from you before then.

FOR YOUR TIME

Dear Jessie,

I wanted to officially thank you for the extra time you took helping us get our newsletter together. You truly went way beyond the call of duty.

The results are wonderful! I've enclosed a copy of the finished product so that you can see your design in its final form. We've already started getting compliments.

Thanks again,

Sincerely,

Alternative Phrases:

- Just a quick note to thank you for all the extra time and effort you took . . .
- Enclosed is a copy of the newsletter you helped us put together. I think you'll be pleased; I know we are. Thank you for all your efforts—they certainly paid off.
- Thank you so much for all the extra time you spent helping with our newsletter.
- We are most pleased with the results.

FOR YOUR HELP

Dear Ed,

We couldn't have done it without you! You helped with so much and made our celebration really work. We're all truly grateful.

Sincerely,

Alternative Phrases:

- We truly appreciate the help you gave us with our celebration. I'm not sure we could have done it without you.
- Our celebration was a success, and much of the credit goes to you. We want to acknowledge and thank you for your efforts.

- Thank you for the work you put into making our celebration a success. It was a pleasure working with you.
- Thank you for the effort you put into making our celebration a success. We specifically appreciated your attention to the flowers and extra lighting.

FOR YOUR SUPPORT—2 LETTERS

TIP: Letters such as the following two have more impact if handwritten.

1.

Dear Bev,

You made such a wonderful difference in yesterday's meeting. I got so caught up in the problem that I almost lost it emotionally. You quietly put the whole situation in perspective.

Thanks for being there and being willing.

Alternative Phrases:

- Thanks for bringing my focus back to the subject at hand during yesterday's meeting.
- I truly appreciated your calmness at yesterday's meeting.

2.

Dear David,

Thanks so much for sticking up for me last week. Even though we didn't get it all our way, your support let us open the door to more possibilities. I felt supported and truly appreciated your efforts.

Sincerely,

Alternative Phrases:

- You were a godsend last week.
- Thanks to your support, we now have more options than before.

THANKS FOR A PRODUCT

Dear Mr. Miller:

I received the replacement tape, "Conversational Selling in Business" today and wanted to let you know that this copy is excellent. So is the material—well worth the time and money.

Thanks for your prompt attention.

Sincerely,

Alternative Phrases:

- Thank you for your prompt replacement of the tape, "Conversational Selling in Business." The quality is excellent and so is the material.
- I really appreciate how quickly you sent me a replacement of . . .
- It's a pleasure doing business with you.

THANKS FOR THE INTRODUCTION

Dear Mr. Miller,

Thanks so much for passing my letter along to Frank Garner. As a result, he gave me a call and we set up a meeting yesterday. Not only did we find a way to do some business together, but we both enjoyed ourselves a lot and are looking forward to a continued association.

Sincerely,

Alternative Phrases:

- Frank Garner gave me a call and we have decided to get together when he's in Washington County next month.
- I'm glad you sent Mr. Garner a copy of my letter to you requesting an introduction.
- I really appreciate your efforts in this matter.

LETTERS OF CONGRATULATIONS

ON YOUR ENGAGEMENT

Dear Ms. Brown,

Congratulations on your recent engagement. We wish you and Mr. Alexander a truly glorious wedding and an even better life together.

As you probably know, our store specializes in service for the bride-to-be. We'd be delighted to help you choose your table settings and carry the information in our Bridal Registry, which can make shopping so much easier for your friends and family.

I've enclosed a few brochures to give you an idea of the lines we carry. If I can be of any service, please call.

Sincerely,

Alternative Phrases:

- Best wishes on your recent engagement to Mr. Alexander. We wish both of you a beautiful wedding and a happy life together.
- Are you aware that our store has specialized in services to brides-to-be for over twenty years?
- Among the services we offer are:
  a bridal registry
  consultation on flatware, glassware, and china coordination
  referrals to dress makers and floral designers

- Enjoy the brochures I've enclosed illustrating some of the many lines we carry.

ON A MARRIAGE

Dear Mr. and Mrs. Watson,

Congratulations on your recent marriage. As a gift to you both, I've enclosed our "Newlyweds Only" certificate, good for a 30 percent discount at any of our locations.

We wish you all the happiness in the world.

Sincerely,

Alternative Phrases:

- Congratulations on your recent nuptials.
- We are pleased to extend our congratulations on your recent marriage.
- Best wishes and may all your dreams come true.

ON A BIRTH

Dear Mr. and Mrs. Sawyer,

Congratulations on the birth of your daughter, Erica. A child is a wonderful addition to a family.

Enclosed is a gift certificate for THE BABY STORE. It's our way of wishing you the best.

Sincerely,

Alternative Phrases:

- The enclosed gift certificate is our way of saying congratulations on the recent addition to your family.
- Congratulations on the recent addition to your family. Please accept the enclosed gift certificate as our way of wishing you the best.
- THE BABY STORE wants to congratulate you on the recent addition to your family. Enclosed is a gift certificate which will not only introduce you to our wonderful line of baby products, but which also expresses our most sincere good wishes.

ON A GRADUATION

Dear Steve,

Congratulations on your recent graduation from Oklahoma State University. We know how hard you worked and are proud to know you.

Sincerely,

Alternative Phrases:

- You made it! We know how hard you worked toward your graduation from Oklahoma State, and your work has paid off.
- We were so delighted to hear of your recent graduation from Oklahoma State. Congratulations. You've made an excellent start.
- Enclosed is a small token as a way of congratulating you on your graduation from Oklahoma State. Keep up the good work; we're proud of you.

ON A CIVIC AWARD

Dear Ms. Wilson:

Congratulations on your "Leucadian of the Year" award. You certainly deserved it. Your contribution to this area through your volunteer work has been outstanding.

Sincerely,

Alternative Phrases:

- No one deserves the "Leucadian of the Year" award more than you. Congratulations.
- I really wasn't surprised to read of your "Leucadian of the Year" award. In fact, it's about time our community recognized the tremendous contribution you have made through your volunteer services. Congratulations.
- Just a note to extend my personal congratulations to you as our "Leucadian of the Year."

ON A SPEECH

Dear Ms. Jeffries:

I was privileged to hear your talk about court reform yesterday before the Bar Association. It was delightful to hear some solutions, as well as a cry of alarm. I particularly liked your ideas about election of judges and want to let you know that I support your efforts.

Sincerely,

Alternative Phrases:

- I was impressed with your talk about court reform at the Bar Association meeting last week.
- Congratulations on your outstanding speech about court reform last week.

- It's about time someone talked about solutions to the judicial problems we have.
- Please add me to your list of supporters.

FOR MENTION IN A PUBLICATION

Dear Ms. Funch:

I was surprised and delighted to see your name listed as a contributing editor to *Chemical Engineering Today.* When we met last week, I had no idea you had such a claim to fame.

Congratulations, and keep writing.

Sincerely,

Alternative Phrases:

- It was with pleasure that I noted your name as a contributing . . .
- Keep up the good work. We need a voice like yours.

ON AN ANNIVERSARY

Dear Mr. and Mrs. Whitman,

Congratulations on your Silver Anniversary. It's wonderful to know that marriages can and do last.

We've enclosed a small gift as a token of our esteem. Use it with our best wishes for your future together.

Sincerely,

Alternative Phrases:

- A silver anniversary is certainly impressive. Congratulations.
- It's couples like you that set an example in these troubled times.
- We wish you many more.

ON A SCHOLARSHIP

Dear Ms. Forseman,

Congratulations on the scholarship awarded to you by the Mill Valley Women's Club. You're obviously a special young lady. We wish you the best of luck at college in September.

Sincerely,

Alternative Phrases:

- I was delighted to hear you had been awarded a scholarship by the Mill Valley Women's Club.
- Your hard work has obviously paid off.
- We are proud to have you represent our community and wish you the best of luck.

ON A NEW HOME

Dear Mr. and Mrs. Sampson:

Congratulations on the purchase of your new home. You're in a wonderful neighborhood and should enjoy both the home and the area for many years to come.

To help you enjoy your new surroundings, we've enclosed a package of special offers from several local businesses. We wish you all the best in your new home.

Sincerely,

Alternative Phrases:

- We want to congratulate you on your recent home purchase and wish you the best.
- The purchase of a home is one of life's highlights and living in your own home one of life's joys.
- The best of luck and happiness with your new home. I'm sure you will enjoy not only your property but the neighborhood, too.

ON YOUR RETIREMENT

Dear Ms. Thompson,

We received word today of your retirement from W.A. Penn and Co. Congratulations. You've worked long and hard and earned a rest. We have enjoyed a rewarding business relationship with you over the years. You will be missed.

Sincerely,

Alternative Phrases:

- Congratulations on your recent retirement from W.A. Penn and Co.
- Your dedication has not gone unnoticed.
- You will be missed.

ON AN EMPLOYMENT ANNIVERSARY

Dear Ms. Riley,

We want to congratulate you for your ten years of employment at Mountain View Services. You've been of tremendous service to us over the years, and we certainly appreciate it. We're looking forward to working with you for many more years.

Sincerely,

Alternative Phrases:

- Congratulations on your tenth anniversary with our firm. The years you've spent with us are truly appreciated.
- We're glad you're part of our firm and look forward to our continuing relationship.
- Please accept this gift as a token of our appreciation.

ON A PROMOTION

Dear Mr. Boyer,

Congratulations on your recent promotion to Sales Manager. We know you'll do a fine job and are looking forward to working with you.

Sincerely,

Alternative Phrases:

- I was delighted to get word of your promotion to Sales Manager. You certainly deserve it, and I know you will do an excellent job.
- Congratulations! They couldn't have picked a better person. Not only do you know your products and your customers, but your ability to motivate the sales staff makes you perfect for the job.

FOR ELECTION TO SERVICE CLUB OFFICE

Dear Sally,

I was delighted to hear you'd been elected president of the Dearborn Boosters Club. Congratulations. I know you'll do an excellent job leading the organization.

Sincerely,

Alternative Phrases:

- Congratulations on your election as president for the Dearborn Boosters Club.
- It was good to hear that the Dearborn Boosters Club had the sense to choose you as their president. Congratulations.
- The organization will benefit from your leadership.

Chapter 8

LETTERS DEALING WITH EMOTIONAL ISSUES

Condolence for the Death of a Child
Sympathy for a Customer's Illness
Sympathy for Illness of a Friend
Sympathy for the Illness of a Family Member

LETTERS ACCOMPANYING GIFTS

Birthday Gift to a Child
Birthday Gift to a Youth
Birthday Gift to a Co-worker
Retirement Gift

LETTERS OF APOLOGY

To Co-worker for Anger
To Co-worker with Offer to Continue Dialog
To Co-worker for Anger but Standing Firm
To Customer for Rudeness
To Customer for Misunderstanding
To Customer for Delay

Many of your letters will deal with concrete situations, but you'll also be called on to write letters dealing with often difficult emotional situations. Such letters can range from writing or replying to a complaint to letters of condolence and sympathy.

Letters that properly handle unhappy or unfortunate situations are important to any business because people are important to business. The goal of these letters is to make the reader feel good, or at least better, about your company. They require tact and deftness of phrasing because you won't always be able to totally satisfy the reader's wants.

Simplicity and truthfulness should be your guide. A simple statement of facts, coupled when possible with a solution, goes a long way toward creating or re-creating good will. Yet even when solutions are not possible, simply letting the reader know that his or her complaint or problem has been heard, and considered, helps greatly. In addition, when making a complaint or delivering unpleasant news, the same approach usually works well.

SECRETARY'S TIPS ON WRITING LETTERS DEALING WITH EMOTIONAL ISSUES

1. *Be sure you understand the purpose of the letter.* If you're answering a complaint, be sure you understand both the nature of the complaint and what solutions, if any, you're in a position to offer. Be clear about the nature of any complaint or bad news that you need to deliver. Your good will and clarity will make the letter easier for you to write and for the reader to understand.
2. *Get all the information you need before composing the letter.* You'll need to know exactly to whom to address the letter, as well as the specifics of the situation you're addressing. For instance, if you're making a complaint, be sure you provide sufficient information for your reader to respond in a helpful

way. If you're delivering bad news, understand why the reader is apt to be unhappy.

3. *Determine the tone of the letter.* Letters dealing with emotional situations should be quiet and calm in tone. The formality or informality will be determined by the nature of the relationship you and your business have with the correspondent.

   Be careful to avoid accusations and blame; such statements contribute nothing to a possible solution and can create even more problems.

4. *The first paragraph should contain the most important information.* The purpose of the letter will determine what actually goes into the first paragraph. Generally, the first paragraph should contain a simple statement about the issues involved. Subsequent information should follow in logical order. If you're also proposing a solution, put that in the first paragraph if possible. If that's not possible, you may be able to at least let the reader know the letter contains a solution.

5. *Make it clear what response, if any, is expected from the reader.* Emotional issues often result in emotional responses. By spelling out just what you expect from the reader, you can often further the cause of understanding and goodwill. Be specific about what sort of a response you want, or let the reader know that no response is desired.

6. *Be concise and complete.* People dealing with emotional situations rarely welcome long letters—there's usually no point in belaboring the issue. On the other hand, you don't want to be so terse or so concise that you sound rude or sound as if the problem isn't fully addressed.

MAKING AND ANSWERING COMPLAINTS

COMPLAINT ABOUT A PRODUCT

Dear Mr. Miller:

I received the tape, "Conversational Selling in Business" today and tried to play it at once. It's hard to tell what happened, but if you listen, you'll be able to tell why I'm unhappy.

I'd like a replacement, and I would appreciate it if you'd try the new tape before you send it to me.

Sincerely,

COMPLAINT ABOUT SERVICE

1.

Dear Sarah:

This is awkward, but we've done business with your firm for years, and I want you to know about a problem. Your new manager, Jerrie Winslow, just doesn't seem to be able to do the job. Three times now we've placed orders for various standard supplies like paper clips, file folders, pens, pencils, and so forth. As usual, we've asked that the orders be delivered. In each case, the delivery hasn't been made when promised—in fact, we've had to call. And when the orders do arrive they're incomplete.

I took the time to go to the store and speak with Ms. Winslow, explaining your usual service for us. She was rude. My sense is that she's just overwhelmed by the job.

I don't know quite what to suggest, but I felt strongly that I should let you know what was happening.

Sincerely,

Alternative Phrases:

- We've been having problems with our orders ever since you hired your new manager, Jerrie Winslow.
- When I spoke to Ms. Winslow, in person, about the problems we were having, she was less than responsive.
- Is it possible she just doesn't understand the job?
- I dislike outlining a problem without also proposing a solution, but in this case I don't know what to suggest.
- We'd like to continue to do business with your store, but unless something changes for the better, we will be forced to look elsewhere for our supplies.

2.

Dear Mr. Tyndale:

I was startled when I came into the office and discovered your usually competent staff had not performed as usual. The ashtrays in the conference room were not emptied, nor was the trash. The bathroom had been given a lick and a promise, but there were spots on the mirror and the bowl wasn't clean. The bookcases were only partially dusted. In short, the office was a mess.

I'd like to continue using your service if possible since, until now, your performance has been excellent. Please let me know how we can avoid such problems in the future.

Sincerely,

Alternative Phrases:

- Something has happened to your usually competent staff. On Tuesday, I came to the office and discovered the ashtrays . . .
- Simply put, the cleaning was unacceptable.
- We'd rather not change cleaning services.
- What can be done to assure this doesn't happen again?

3.

Dear Sir/Madam:

The last two weeks we have not received the bottled water we're scheduled for. I called your office following the first missed delivery and was assured that our water would be delivered and that we'd be put back on the schedule. But that hasn't happened. How can we get this straightened out?

Very truly yours,

Alternative Phrases:

- We have not received our bottled water for two weeks.
- Although your office assured me our water would be delivered, it hasn't been.
- What do we need to do?

RESPONSE TO A COMPLAINT—YOU'RE RIGHT

1.

Dear Katherine:

I'm so glad you felt comfortable writing me about the problems you've had with my manager Jerrie Winslow. You are absolutely right, she's been totally overwhelmed by the job.

But we've evolved a plan that I think will work. For the next 30 days, I will be in the store with her from 10:00 in the morning until about 3:00 in the afternoon. As a result of this, we both expect her to develop a better feeling for the way I want the business conducted. Of course, we may discover that she just won't work out, in which case I'll replace her.

Thanks again for your input, and I hope this solution means you'll continue to do business with us.

Sincerely,

Alternative Phrases:

- I am truly sorry you've been having problems with my manager and am glad you felt free to let me know what's been happening.
- When I talked with her, I discovered she just didn't understand what I wanted.

- Please be assured I will take whatever action is necessary to get the store back to "business as usual."

2.

Dear Ms. Browning:

I'm so sorry your office was not cleaned properly, and I appreciate your telling me about it. As it happens, we had hired an extra crew, and I'm afraid I made a mistake in my choice. The problem crew has been replaced, and I've adjusted your bill to reflect no charge for the improper cleaning.

If you have any problem in the future, please feel free to call me at once. We can usually get the problem solved the same day we hear from you.

Sincerely,

Alternative Phrases:

- Thank you for letting me know about the poor cleaning job.
- Our business is expanding, and I've been hiring new people. Obviously, I chose the wrong ones.
- We won't, of course, charge you for the poor job.
- I've changed the way I'm assigning new people to make sure they learn the ropes from our experienced personnel.

3.

Dear Ms. Gibson:

You're absolutely right—we've had nothing but problems with our water delivery in your area during the past few weeks. I can only apologize and let you know we've taken action to solve the problem.

We have a new driver and a new receptionist. I've made sure both of them know your name and the name of your firm. Your deliveries should be on time in the future.

As an additional way to express our concern, I've enclosed a discount coupon for a pound of coffee.

Sincerely,

Alternative Phrases:

- I'm so sorry you haven't been receiving your water. We've had problems in your area, but I think we've got them straightened out.
- I've replaced some of our people, and that should solve the problem.
- Please accept the enclosed discount coupon as a token of my apology.

RESPONSE TO A COMPLAINT—YOU'RE WRONG

1.

Dear Katherine:

I'm so glad you felt comfortable writing me about the problems you've had with your recent orders. I've talked with my manager, and she tells me there was some real confusion in the way the orders were placed. As near as I can tell, someone new in your office gave us a call. Apparently, he or she didn't have the catalog at hand and was unable to give us the proper order numbers. Nor was that person clear on the quantities to be ordered. In each case, there was one item that required special handling, which delayed the delivery. Perhaps we didn't make that clear.

In any event, enclosed is a new copy of our catalog. I've also made some extra copies of the order blank and hope that whoever places the order will take time to fill one out before they make the call.

We value your business and expect this will solve the problem. If not, please give me a call.

Sincerely,

Alternative Phrases:

- I think most of the ordering problems you've had with us recently have originated in your office. As near as I can tell, someone new . . .
- You may want to remind your people that we need the proper order numbers and the quantity of each item. Special orders may delay delivery.

- Enclosed is a new copy of our catalog and a supply of order blanks. If the blanks are filled out before the call is placed, the process will go smoothly.
- Let me know if this doesn't solve the problem.

2.

Dear Ms. Browning:

I'm so sorry you feel your office was not cleaned properly, and I appreciate your telling me about it. I checked with our cleaning crew—it was the usual one—and they tell me that just as they were getting started, three people came into the conference room. Our guess is that there was a late meeting that you're not aware of.

Perhaps we need to schedule the cleanings for later in the evening, or perhaps we need to schedule an extra cleaning when you have special, late meetings. Be assured that our goal is the same as yours: a clean office that properly represents your business.

Please give me a call, and we'll see what we can do to solve the problem.

Sincerely,

Alternative Phrases:

- You may not be aware of it, but our cleaning people were forced to leave the conference room in the middle of their cleaning when three members of your staff arrived for a late meeting.
- Could I suggest that you let us know when late meetings are planned so that we can adjust our schedule to match yours?
- As you know from our past performance, it's our intention to give you the service you want and deserve.

3.

Dear Ms. Gibson:

Something doesn't make sense—our delivery man shows he made the usual water delivery on the dates you say you didn't receive the water.

He does show that on those dates your office was locked and that he had to leave the water in the hall, which is what we've been doing in that situation all along.

Since he's been on the route for several years and since we haven't had any other complaints from his route, I have to assume something's wrong at your end. I know your office is often locked—is there someone nearby we could leave the water with?

Please give me a call so that we can figure out what needs to be done. By the way, we won't bill you for the missing water.

Sincerely,

Alternative Phrases:

- Our records show that water was actually delivered on the dates you question.
- As requested in your instructions, he left the water outside your door since your office was locked.
- Perhaps you can make arrangements to have someone on site to receive the water.
- Let me know how you want to handle this.

COMPLAINT ABOUT PARKING SPACE

Dear Sir/Madam:

Can you help us? For the past week or so, several of your employees have been parking directly in front of our store—which means our customers have to hunt for parking. We've posted three of the spaces, but with no results.

Sincerely,

Alternative Phrases:

- In spite of proper posting, several of your employees are parking directly in front of our store—which means our customers have to find parking elsewhere.
- Our customers are not able to use the three posted parking spaces in front of our store because several of your employees are parking there on a regular basis.
- Would you please notify your staff that we will be forced to enforce towing if we find their cars in our spaces?

RESPONSE TO COMPLAINT ABOUT PARKING

1.

Dear Ms. Johnson:

Thanks for bringing your problem with our employees to our attention. Enclosed is a copy of the memo I've circulated which should help. If you discover one of our people parked in front of your store, please get the license number of the car and give me a call. We'll ask them to move.

Very truly yours,

Alternative Phrases:

- We've circulated the attached memo to our employees about your parking spaces.
- We maintain a license plate file on our staff and can quickly determine if the cars in your parking spaces belong to our people. If you give us a call, we'll make sure they move.
- If the memo doesn't help, then go ahead and call the towing company.

2.

Dear Ms. Johnson:

Although we'd like to honor your request about our employees parking in front of your store, we can't until the construction is completed in the back of the building. I checked with the landlord, and he assures me seven parking spaces will be freed up by next Monday. This Friday I'll circulate a memo to our people alerting them to the parking in back.

Very truly yours,

Alternative Phrases:

- I'm sorry about our violation of your parking spaces—it's been caused by the construction at the back of the building.
- The landlord has promised to make seven spaces available in back by next week.
- We'll let our people know about the additional parking this Friday.

LETTERS CONVEYING BAD NEWS

CANCELING A SPEAKING ENGAGEMENT

1.

Dear Ms. Garth:

Mr. Thomas Hemming has asked me to inform you that a family illness will prevent him from speaking to your group on July 11. At this point it is impossible to tell when Mr. Hemming will be available for speaking engagements again.

We appreciate the opportunity and are genuinely sorry for the inconvenience.

Sincerely,

Alternative Phrases:

- I'm sorry to have to inform you that Mr. Hemming is forced to cancel his speaking engagement with your group due to a family illness.

- We expect he will be able to resume speaking in about two weeks.
- May we suggest Robert Planck as an alternate? You may contact him at 555-7223.
- Thank you for your understanding in this situation.

2.

Dear Mr. Kraemer:

An unavoidable conflict has occurred in my speaking schedule, which means I won't be able to talk to your group on April 17. I could, however, speak on April 21. Please think about it, and I'll give you a call next week.

Sincerely,

Alternative Phrases:

- Because of unforeseen events, I will be unable to speak before your group on April 17 as scheduled.
- My next available speaking dates are April 21 and May 5. If any of these would work for you please let me know.
- I'm sorry for the inconvenience this causes.

ANNOUNCING THE HOSPITALIZATION OF A STAFF MEMBER—INTRODUCING A TEMPORARY EMPLOYEE

Dear Jean:

We're sorry to inform you that Paul Benzer in Systems Development has been hospitalized. We anticipate that he will be in the hospital for two weeks and will spend at least six weeks recuperating at home.

In the meantime, Robin Schwartz will be filling in.

If you'd like to send a card to Paul, he is at the Watford Community Hospital in Watford, Pennsylvania.

Sincerely,

Alternative Phrases:

- You may already be aware that Paul Benzer in Systems Development is in the hospital. We are happy to report he is recovering nicely and expects to be home for recuperation by January 20 and back to work by March 16.
- Robin Schwartz will be filling in during the interim.
- You may send cards to Paul at . . .
- Paul has asked that cards and flowers not be sent at this time.

ANNOUNCING THE HOSPITALIZATION OF A STAFF MEMBER WHO WILL BE REPLACED

Dear George:

As you may have heard, Barbara Mann was hospitalized last week. We're sorry to tell you that her illness will be a long one, which means we will have to hire someone to take her place.

In the meantime, if you'd like to send a card or flowers, Barbara is in Room 417 at Tioga County Hospital.

Sincerely,

Alternative Phrases:

- We're sorry to announce that Barbara Mann in Sales was taken ill and is in the hospital. Unfortunately, her illness is likely to be protracted and she has suggested we replace her.
- We will be interviewing and expect to hire someone within the next two weeks.
- Barbara would appreciate cards and letters, but not flowers. They may be sent to . . .

ANNOUNCING THE DEATH OF A STAFF MEMBER

1.

Dear Colleagues:

You may have heard that one of our vice-presidents, Jack Bescham, died last night after a short illness. We'll all miss him.

The company will hold a memorial service at Chapel-by-the-Sea, 175 Pacific View in Cardiff, on November 2 at 11:00 A.M. The offices will be closed so that everyone can attend.

Alternative Phrases:

- Jack Bescham, our vice-president, died suddenly last night.
- He will be sorely missed by all.
- We will close the offices on November 2 so those who choose can attend the memorial services. The services will be held at Chapel-by-the-Sea, 175 Pacific View in Cardiff.

2.

Dear Colleagues:

We are sad to announce that our comptroller, Angel Martiniz, passed away last week. The family has elected to hold a private funeral service. However, we will hold a brief memorial service at 10:00 A.M. on May 10 at Memorial Chapel.

The family has also asked that instead of flowers, donations be sent to the American Heart Association.

We'll all miss Angel.

Sincerely,

Alternative Phrases:

- We are sorry to tell you that our comptroller, Angel Martiniz, died last week.

- We are sorry to announce the death of . . .
- The company will hold a memorial service on . . .
- Mr. Martinez will be missed by us all.

PRODUCT NO LONGER AVAILABLE—REFUND ENCLOSED

Dear Ms. Brown:

We're sorry to inform you that we are not able to deliver the leather sandals you ordered because they are no longer being made.

Enclosed is a full refund, including the postage and handling charge. We are also enclosing a copy of our new catalog in hopes you may find something else you'd like to order from us.

Sincerely,

Alternative Phrases:

- Thank you for your order. However, the leather sandals are no longer being made, so we will not be able to send them to you.
- We are refunding your purchase price, plus postage and handling, for the leather sandals you ordered from us. The sandals are no longer available.
- The new catalog, which is enclosed, is full of items that are available.

PRODUCT NO LONGER AVAILABLE—SENDING A SUBSTITUTE

Dear Mr. Sanchez:

It doesn't seem possible, but we are no longer able to supply our usual line of camel's hair brushes. However, we have been able to locate another line which we feel are at least as good. So we have taken the liberty of filling your order with the new line; you should be receiving them soon.

Thanks so much for your understanding.

Sincerely,

Alternative Phrases:

- We are so sorry to tell you we are no longer able to supply the camel's hair brushes you ordered, but we have found another line which is at least as good.
- We'd like you to try our new line, so we have filled your order with those. If they are not satisfactory, please don't hesitate to return them for a full refund.
- We expect you'll find them as good, or perhaps even better, than the old line.

PRODUCT AVAILABLE, BUT COSTS MORE

Dear Bill:

Thanks so much for your inquiry about our radial sails. Since we last talked, we've sold several suits and the owners are most happy with their choice.

However, our cloth suppliers have recently informed us that the dacron we used has increased in price. This means the cost of the sails you asked about will be 15 percent higher than the price we talked about last month.

Because the cloth prices seem to be going up at regular intervals, I hope you can place your order soon. We can only guarantee this price for 60 days.

Sincerely,

Alternative Phrases:

- Dear Mr. Hogan:
- It pains me to inform you that the price of cloth for the dacron sails we discussed has gone up in price. Assuming the parameters are the same, the sails will cost $1,500 instead of $1,380.
- Cloth prices seem to be going up rapidly right now, so you may want to place your order soon to hold the price.

LETTERS OF CONDOLENCE AND SYMPATHY

CONDOLENCE FOR THE DEATH OF A SPOUSE

Dear Mrs. Bryant,

We were so sorry to hear of Harold's death and wish there were something we could say that would help ease your grief.

If there's any way we can be of service, please give us a call.

Sincerely,

Alternative Phrases:

- We were shocked and sorrowed to hear of Mr. Bryant's death.
- We know there is nothing we can say to make this easier for you, but please know you have our deepest sympathy.
- Don't hesitate to contact us if we can be of any help during this most difficult time.

CONDOLENCE FOR THE DEATH OF A PARENT

Dear Kathy,

I was so sorry to hear about the death of your mother, Mary Beth. What a shock for you! She was a truly beautiful person and will be missed by all of us. I wish there were something I could say that would make this time easier for you.

If I can help in any way, please call.

Sincerely,

Alternative Phrases:

- Please accept my deepest sympathy for the loss of your mother, Mary Beth Rubin.
- This must be such a difficult time for you.
- Know that we too will miss her.

CONDOLENCE FOR THE DEATH OF A CHILD

Dear Catherine and David,

We were shocked to hear of the death of your daughter, Annette. The loss of a child is a horrible thing. Know that our thoughts and prayers are with you.

Sincerely,

Alternative Phrases:

- Dear Mr. and Mrs. Johnson,
- Please accept our sincerest condolences.
- Know that our best wishes and thoughts are with you during this time.

SYMPATHY FOR A CUSTOMER'S ILLNESS

Dear Jeff,

We heard about your surgery and wanted to let you know how glad we are it went well. It's not an easy thing to go through by any means.

Sincerely,

Alternative Phrases:

- Congratulations on your successful surgery.
- We are sorry to hear about your illness.
- Any illness is unpleasant and difficult. We're glad to hear you're on the mend.

SYMPATHY FOR THE ILLNESS OF A FRIEND

Dear Tyler,

Good heavens! I didn't know you were in the hospital until today. Sue told me about your ordeal and says you're getting along well. She also tells me visitors aren't appropriate for another week, so I won't stop by until them.

If you need anything in the meantime, give me a call.

Best wishes,

Alternative Phrases:

- I was surprised to hear you were in the hospital. However, Sue tells me you're doing well.
- I know you can't have visitors, but I did want you to know I'm thinking about you and sending you good thoughts.
- Please have someone let me know as soon as you want visitors.

SYMPATHY FOR THE ILLNESS OF A FAMILY MEMBER

Dear Anne,

I'm so sorry that your mother is seriously ill. This must be a particularly difficult time for you. Is there anything I can do? If there is, please let me know.

Love,

Alternative Phrases:

- I heard today that your mother is ill, and I wanted to let you know how sorry I am.
- My best wishes are with you in this difficult time.
- Please let me know if I can help in any way.

LETTERS ACCOMPANYING GIFTS

BIRTHDAY GIFT TO A CHILD

Dear Tanya,

A special happy birthday for a special girl. It's such fun to watch you as you grow up.

Your friend,

Alternative Phrases:

- I wanted to wish you a very happy birthday.
- You're growing up to be a beautiful young lady.
- The enclosed is a token of our affection for you.
- Sincerely,

BIRTHDAY GIFT TO A YOUTH

Dear Steve,

Happy Birthday. Eighteen is an important age for many reasons. The most obvious is the official recognition of your adult status.

We hope you enjoy the enclosed book.

Sincerely,

Alternative Phrases:

- Welcome to the world of adulthood, and happy birthday on this special day.
- Please know that the gift is a token of my affection for you.

BIRTHDAY GIFT TO A CO-WORKER

Dear Gayle,

It's such a pleasure to work with you, and I wanted to acknowledge you on your birthday.

Best wishes,

Alternative Phrases:

- I truly enjoy working with you and wanted to wish you a special happy birthday.
- Happy birthday to a wonderful co-worker. You deserve the best.

RETIREMENT GIFT

Dear John,

It doesn't seem possible that you're retiring. It's been such a pleasure working with you. Thanks so much for all you've taught me and for your infinite patience.

Sincerely,

Alternative Phrases:

- Congratulations on your retirement.
- I'm going to miss you around here.

- You've taught me so much and have been so patient—it just won't be the same.

LETTERS OF APOLOGY

TO CO-WORKER FOR ANGER

Highly personal letters of apology are often more effective when handwritten.

Dear Regina,

I'm so very sorry I got so angry yesterday. You deserve better treatment from me.

Sincerely,

Alternative Phrases:

- I can only apologize for my outburst yesterday.
- You did nothing to deserve becoming the object of my anger.
- Please forgive me for my anger at you yesterday.

TIP: TO CO-WORKER WITH OFFER TO CONTINUE DIALOG

Dear Tom:

Please forgive me for my anger yesterday. I find this project frustrating, but that's no excuse for me to take my frustration out on you.

Part of my frustration comes because I feel so strongly, yet I know I haven't given your ideas a fair hearing. Could we talk a bit more?

Sincerely,

Alternative Phrases:

- I'm sorry I got so upset yesterday—you don't deserve that sort of treatment.
- My feelings about this project are strong, but I could probably learn a lot by listening to your ideas.
- Would you be willing to try discussing this with me again?

TO CO-WORKER FOR ANGER BUT STANDING FIRM

Dear Mr. Wilder,

My display of anger yesterday was inexcusable, and I can only apologize. However, I do want to go on record as being opposed to your proposal. As you know, I feel there are more efficient ways to accomplish the same task. I would appreciate it if you'd give the attached your consideration.

Sincerely,

Alternative Phrases:

- I'm truly sorry I lost my temper yesterday.
- Although I wished I had expressed it differently, I am extremely uncomfortable with your proposal.
- The attached memo outlines not only some specific suggestions, but also the reasons behind them.

TO CUSTOMER—FOR RUDENESS

Dear Mr. Johnson:

Please accept my sincerest apologies for the poor treatment you received in our reception area yesterday. We've taken steps to make sure it doesn't happen again.

Sincerely,

Alternative Phrases:

- Your treatment in our reception room yesterday was inexcusable. Please accept my apologies.
- Be assured we've made the changes necessary to assure such treatment isn't repeated.

TO CUSTOMER FOR MISUNDERSTANDING

Dear Ms. Wilcox:

I wanted to let you know that I'm really sorry for the misunderstanding that resulted in your having to spend the better part of the day in our offices trying to get it straightened out. If it's any comfort to you, as a result of what happened, we've plugged an important hole in our procedures. Thank you for your willingness to hang in there.

Sincerely,

Alternative Phrases:

- Please accept my apologies for the misunderstanding yesterday.
- I'm sorry you had to spend so much time trying to get the misunderstanding straightened out.
- We've taken steps to make sure this sort of thing doesn't happen again.

TO CUSTOMER FOR DELAY

Dear Mr. Kitcher,

Your letter, dated April 4, just came to my attention. I'm not sure why it took so long to surface, and I hope you'll excuse the delay.

Enclosed is the information you requested.

Sincerely,

Alternative Phrases:

- I don't know how it happened, but your letter of April 4 just surfaced.
- Please forgive us for this inexcusable delay.
- At last, the information you requested is enclosed.

Chapter 9

LETTERS IN THE PUBLIC SECTOR

LETTERS TO PUBLIC OFFICIALS

To The Mayor Regarding an Outstanding Employee
To Community Traffic Control Regarding Dangerous Intersection
To Local Law Enforcement Regarding Vandalism, Vagrancy
To Zoning Commission Regarding Proposed Zoning Change
To City Council Member Regarding Proposed Zoning Change
To Assessor Regarding Property Tax Increase
To County Board of Supervisors—Thanks for Help
To a Member of Congress in Support of Legislation

LETTERS REGARDING POLITICAL CAMPAIGNS

Agreeing to be Associated with a Candidate
Endorsing a Candidate
Refusing to Be Associated with a Candidate

LETTERS REGARDING PUBLIC CAUSES

Agreeing to Be Associated with a Cause
Endorsing a Cause
Refusing to Endorse a Cause

Every business is part of a larger community and as such must deal with the public sector. This means there are many occasions for writing letters to public officials.

Although letters to public officials are similar to other business letters, they are different in one respect: often, you're dealing directly with matters of law. For this reason, such letters must be written with even more care, and careful records must be kept.

Every area of the country has public officials dealing with almost every aspect of business. If you're not sure of whom to write to, you may be able to find out by calling your local newspaper. Many telephone directories also carry a listing of government offices, and some have a general information number for local government. Also, your letter will be more effective if you can get the name (double check the spelling) of the official as well as the office.

SECRETARY'S TIPS ON WRITING LETTERS TO PUBLIC OFFICIALS

1. *Be sure you understand the purpose of the letter.* You must be clear on the purpose of your letter when writing to public officials. Each official is extremely busy, and your letter will probably be routed through channels, making clarity of purpose an utmost necessity.
2. *Get all the information you need before composing the letter.* The more complete your information, the more accurate and understandable your letter will be. Since the chances are that your letter will be opened and read by someone who isn't familiar with the situation, complete information is necessary in order to get an appropriate response.

   Forms of address are important when dealing with public officials and many dictionaries provide complete information. Your local librarian can also help you determine exactly how to address the official in question.

3. *Determine the tone of the letter.* Keep your letter simple and neutral in tone. Complex or inflammatory language is apt to cause more problems than it solves.
4. *The first paragraph should contain the most important information.* Because the people reading your letter are busy and possibly unfamiliar with your topic, your first paragraph must give them a reasonable overview of the subject. Subsequent paragraphs should develop the topic more thoroughly.
5. *Make it clear what response, if any, is expected from the reader.* Let the recipient know what sort of response you expect. If you need information, ask for it. If you're asking someone to take a particular action, ask them to let you know what was done and when it was done. On the other hand, if you're just making a comment or giving information and you need no response, say so.
6. *Be concise and complete.* Conciseness and completeness may be more important when writing letters to government officials than in any other area of business. The better job you do writing, the more likely you are to get the response you want.

LETTERS TO PUBLIC OFFICIALS

TO THE MAYOR REGARDING AN OUTSTANDING EMPLOYEE

Dear Mayor Hutchings:

We'd like to draw your attention to an outstanding city employee. Lee Whitman has been driving the sanitation truck in our area for at least five years and has often gone beyond the normal call of duty.

Last week was a particularly good example. We had received two new computers, their peripherals, and some computer furniture. All of it came in good-sized boxes. We were actually in the process of breaking them down when Lee came by to pick up our trash. He immediately began to help, and we hadn't even asked.

We certainly appreciate his attitude, and are sure you will too.

Sincerely,

Alternative Phrases:

- In this time when people seem to be complaining about public employees, I would like to point out a man who is doing an excellent job.
- . . . and can be counted on for extra service gladly given.
- For example, last week we had received . . .
- Lee sets a good example for us all.

TO COMMUNITY TRAFFIC CONTROL REGARDING DANGEROUS INTERSECTION

Dear Mr. Taylor:

We'd like to add our plea to putting in a traffic light, or at least a four-way stop, at the intersection of Ebbtide and Marinship. Just yesterday, one of our employees was involved in a minor collision, largely because so many north-bound people are trying to turn left on Marinship.

We hope you will see your way clear to take action before a serious accident occurs.

Sincerely,

Alternative Phrases:

- Please count us among those who recognize the need for a traffic light, or at least a four-way . . .
- One of our staff was involved in a minor accident there only yesterday. The cause really seemed to be the large number of north-bound . . .

- If something isn't done soon, there will be a serious, possibly fatal accident.

TO LOCAL LAW ENFORCEMENT REGARDING VANDALISM, VAGRANCY

Dear Sheriff Joynson:

We're sure you're aware of the increase in transient traffic and the associated problems at the dock known as the COOP in Sausalito. Is there nothing that can be done to eliminate or reduce the problem?

Our offices back up to that area, and we're constantly faced with vandalism to cars, extra trash pick-up, and strange characters lurking in the parking lot.

Each time we've had a problem, we've called your emergency number. Your officers have arrived promptly most of the time and have done a good job when they got there. However, we know your people can't be nearby all the time, and we feel it would be better for all concerned if a more permanent solution could be found.

Sincerely,

Alternative Phrases:

- What has to happen to eliminate or significantly reduce the problems associated with the transient traffic at the COOP dock downtown?
- We're forced to report acts of vandalism, call for extra trash pick-up, or keep an eye on strangers in the parking lot on at least a weekly basis.
- Although your officers are generally quick to arrive when we call, it seems as if a lot of time and money is being wasted. We'd like to see a more permanent solution. For instance, can't some of these people be picked up for vagrancy?

TO ZONING COMMISSION REGARDING PROPOSED ZONING CHANGE

Dear Director Smith:

We'd like to officially protest the contemplated change in zoning along Elm Avenue between 1001 and 3500 from R-1 to R-3. As we understand the proposed change, this would increase the density from one unit per lot to three units per lot.

Although we recognize the need for more housing in our community, this is certainly the wrong area for it. From the standpoint of our business, the primary problem is parking. The nature of the hillside in this area is that it won't allow off-street parking without tremendous expense. Our employees and clients have great difficulty finding parking nearby as it is. Additional housing will certainly make a bad problem even worse.

We're sure that there are more creative ways to begin to meet the need for housing.

Sincerely,

Alternative Phrases:

- We are totally opposed to the proposed change in zoning along Elm Avenue . . .
- Although changing the density from one unit to three units per lot would increase the housing potential, this is the wrong area.
- While lack of adequate parking is the most obvious problem, the added number of people will probably have the worst long-term effects.
- There is no reason to use this area to create additional housing units when much more suitable locations are available.

TO CITY COUNCIL MEMBER REGARDING PROPOSED ZONING CHANGE

Dear Council Member Jeffries:

Enclosed is a copy of a letter I sent to Hal Smith registering my protest about the proposed zoning change on Elm Avenue.

Thank you for your time and interest.

Sincerely,

Alternative Phrases:

- The enclosed is a copy of a letter I sent to Hal Smith to register my protest . . .
- Please add my voice to the opposition about the proposed zoning change on Elm Avenue. Enclosed is a copy . . .
- I would appreciate it if you would take a public stand against this change.

TO ASSESSOR REGARDING PROPERTY TAX INCREASE

Dear Assessor James:

We received the notice showing our properties' recent evaluation for property tax, and we find the increase unreasonable.

Please send the information we need to file an official protest immediately.

Sincerely,

Alternative Phrases:

- We intend to protest the recent re-evaluation of our properties. We can find no justification for the proposed increase and subsequent raise in property tax.

- Please send me information on filing a protest against the recent re-evaluation. We find our increase unreasonable and intend to take whatever recourse is available to us.
- Although we recognize that our properties have increased in value, we feel your re-evaluation is excessive.

TO COUNTY BOARD OF SUPERVISORS—THANKS FOR HELP

Dear Supervisor Taylor:

I wanted to thank you for your efforts on behalf of getting a county airport located in Fallbrook. It didn't work this time, but we came close, and your work brought us closer than I expected.

Thank you for your time and interest.

Sincerely,

Alternative Phrases:

- I can't thank you enough for your help in trying to get an airport located in Fallbrook.
- I'm sorry we weren't successful this time, but with your help I'm sure we'll make it next time.

TO A MEMBER OF CONGRESS IN SUPPORT OF LEGISLATION

Dear Senator Small:

We at Southern Manufacturing, Inc. are writing in support of resolution #SR10973. This resolution, recognizing National Secretaries' Week, would go a long way towards showing our support staffs respect and appreciation for a job well done.

We hope we can count on your support and appreciate your efforts in making National Secretaries' Week a reality.

Respectfully yours,

LETTERS REGARDING POLITICAL CAMPAIGNS

AGREEING TO BE ASSOCIATED WITH A CANDIDATE

Dear Peter,

Yes, you may use my name on your campaign literature and letterhead. I like your ideas and think you'd make a refreshing change.

Sincerely,

Alternative Phrases:

- I'd be delighted to have my name appear on your campaign literature and letterhead.
- I've listened to you talk and read your policy statement and would be pleased to have my name associated with you and your campaign.
- Yes, you may use my name, but could I see a copy of the ad before it appears?

ENDORSING A CANDIDATE

Dear Ms. Rose:

I'm pleased to give my official endorsement to your campaign for City Council, both as a private citizen and in my position as FHA President.

Sincerely,

Alternative Phrases:

- As an Allenville resident, I'm not only happy to give you my official endorsement, but would be willing to do some work on your campaign.
- Thank you for considering me important enough to ask for an endorsement. My answer is an unqualified YES.

- You may use my name on your campaign literature as a private person; however, the FHA is not taking a position on candidates this year, so we'll have to leave that out.

REFUSING TO BE ASSOCIATED WITH A CANDIDATE

Dear Mr. Seashore:

Thank you for asking me to be associated with your campaign; however, I must decline. As you're probably aware, I've given an endorsement to Peter Kraemer.

Best of luck and may the best person win.

Sincerely,

Alternative Phrases:

- I must refuse your request to officially associate my name with your candidacy for City Council.
- I'm sure you're aware, you and I have some serious disagreements about how to develop or not develop the waterfront.
- Thank you for asking.

LETTERS REGARDING PUBLIC CAUSES

AGREEING TO BE ASSOCIATED WITH A CAUSE

Dear Mr. Greg:

Thanks for the information on your group. Yes, I'd definitely like to be associated with your efforts, both by name and by offering some computer assistance if you need it. My home phone is 555-3789. I look forward to hearing from you.

Sincerely,

Alternative Phrases:

- After looking over your literature and talking with you, I've decided that I'd feel privileged to be associated with your cause.
- Not only may you use my name on your literature, but also I may be able to help you set up your computer database.
- Please feel free to call me at home, 555-3789.

ENDORSING A CAUSE

Dear Mr. Greg:

I'm delighted to give you my endorsement of your cause. It seems to me that in a very complex situation you and your group are proposing a viable solution. Please feel free to use my name on your letterhead, literature, etc.

Sincerely,

Alternative Phrases:

- Yes, you may use my name on your literature, letterhead, and so on.
- The solution your group is proposing seems fair to all concerned.

REFUSING TO ENDORSE A CAUSE

1.

Dear Mr. Greg:

No, I cannot bring myself to endorse your cause, although I am in sympathy with your position. There are too many questions yet to be answered. I would, however, appreciate it if you'd keep me posted.

Truly yours,

Alternative Phrases:

- Although I understand your position, there are too many unanswered questions for me to feel comfortable endorsing your cause.
- I would consider endorsing your cause only if you could assure me that your plan would eliminate *all* excessive tariffs on foreign goods. Since that isn't possible at the moment, I'll have to refuse.
- I know this situation is changing constantly and would like to be kept on your mailing list.

2.

Dear Mr. Greg:

Given the situation, there is no way I can endorse your cause. Although I agree a compromise is necessary, I feel your solution would only make the problem worse.

Sincerely,

Alternative Phrases:

- I'm surprised you've asked for my endorsement. I thought my position in opposition to yours was clear.
- While I recognize the effort that went into your compromise position paper, I don't feel such a compromise is appropriate. Since I am opposed to what you're trying to do, I cannot offer any endorsement or even any encouragement.

Chapter 10

LETTERS FOR NON-PROFIT ORGANIZATIONS

LETTERS FOR NON-PROFIT CORPORATIONS

Answering Request for Information
Requesting Information about an Organization
Request for Donations (series of 3)
Acknowledging Donation
Announcing Event
Request to Serve on Board (series of 2)
Enclosure of Donation Records
Invitation to Meet the President
Request to Head a Committee
Volunteer Opportunities (series of 2)
Refusing Membership in an Organization
Applying for Membership

The staffs of most non-profit organizations are made up of both paid professionals and unpaid volunteers. Working with volunteers presents a challenge to such organizations. In many such offices, volunteers are responsible for generating letters. Yet the business experience of such volunteers is mixed, and they may need more detailed instructions than paid workers. Thus, maintaining a file of typical letters can be particularly helpful in non-profit organizations.

SECRETARY'S TIPS ON WRITING LETTERS FOR NON-PROFIT ORGANIZATIONS

1. *Be sure you understand the purpose of the letter.* Make sure the purpose of the letter is clear. For instance, are you answering a request for information? If so, exactly what sort of information should the letter contain? Are you sending donation records? What period do they cover? Be certain you know exactly what purpose your letter will serve.
2. *Get all the information you need before composing the letter.* Although you may have sufficient information in your head to generate the letter, write it down. The time spent making sure all the information needed is available will be more than saved by avoiding correcting mistakes.
3. *Determine the tone of the letter.* Set a business-like tone for all your correspondence. Letters that require a less formal or more formal tone than usual should probably be generated by a professional rather than by a volunteer. Fundraising letters should also be composed by a professional staff member.
4. *The first paragraph should contain the most important information.* The first paragraph of the letter should let the recipient know what it's about. Most simple letters for non-profit

organizations can be kept to a paragraph or two, making it easier to keep the important information up front.

5. *Make it clear what response, if any, is expected from the reader.* Are you expecting a response from the recipient? If you are, tell him or her exactly what response you need, and how he or she should communicate with you. If no response is expected, make that clear so that you can avoid unnecessary phone calls or correspondence.
6. *Be concise and complete.* Many nonprofit organizations send letters, and if yours are concise and complete, you're more likely to get the response you want.

LETTERS FOR NON-PROFIT CORPORATIONS

ANSWERING REQUEST FOR INFORMATION

Dear Mr. Jameson:

Thank you for your request for information about exhibiting in the Palmyra Art Festival. We have several opportunities for artists to exhibit their works during the Twenty-first Annual Celebration. I've enclosed three brochures. "Artist Exhibitors" contains the information you will need to exhibit your work. The other two contain general information about the festival and about the area.

Sincerely,

Alternative Phrases:

- The enclosed brochures should answer your questions about the Twenty-first Annual Palmyra Art Festival.
- We'd be pleased to consider your art work for the Twenty-first Annual Palmyra Art Festival. I've enclosed . . .
- Enclosed is the information you requested about exhibiting in this year's Palmyra Art Festival.

REQUESTING INFORMATION ABOUT AN ORGANIZATION

Dear Sir/Madam:

I saw the article referring to your organization in the *Independent Press Journal,* and I'd like more information.

Thank you,

Alternative Phrases:

- I understand yours is the organization trying to protect wetlands nationwide. Could you send me more information?
- I'd like information about your organization.
- Please send me information about your organization.

REQUEST FOR DONATIONS

1.

(Today's date)

Dear Mill Valley Resident:

The library needs your help. Over the July 4th weekend, a water pipe broke in the library. Because of the holiday, it wasn't discovered for two days, which meant a tremendous amount of water leaked out. The carpets were soaked and damage was done to book shelves.

With the help of the fire department, we were able to drain the water, but we were forced to pull up the carpet because it couldn't be dried in time to prevent mold damage to the books.

We also have to remove twenty-five book cases. Ten of these can be repaired, but fifteen will have to be replaced.

As you might guess, all this has been expensive, and our insurance covers only part of the repair costs. In order to complete the repair on the book cases, replace the carpet, and pay for the storage of several thousand books, we need your financial help.

The enclosed postage-paid envelope will make your contribution easy. Please send what you can as soon as you can.

Sincerely,

Alternative Phrases:

- You probably know that over the July 4th weekend the library was flooded due to a broken water main. As a result, we need your help.
- The water was removed, thanks to the fire department, but we were forced . . .
- We've already spent the amount our insurance provides.
- Please use the enclosed postage-paid envelope to make your tax-deductible contribution. Your generosity will be appreciated.

2.

Dear Ms. Stevens:

It's time to renew your membership in listener-supported public radio station, KCRW.

The enclosed brochure lists the premiums available during this year's campaign. Additionally, members who renew before September 1 will receive an enameled KCRW pin.

Thank you for your continued support.

Alternative Phrases:

- It's membership renewal time at KCRW, your listener-supported public radio station.
- As usual, we have intriguing gifts for our supporters—the enclosed brochure explains them in detail.
- As a special gift, we will send a beautiful enameled KCRW pin to those who renew before September 1.
- Your continued support is appreciated.

3.

Dear Mill Valley Resident,

Over the years you've come to expect the highest level of care from Valley General Hospital. In order to continue to provide our community with the best medical service possible, our board of directors has recommended acquisition of a nuclear magnetic resonator (NMR).

NMR is an advanced, noninvasive diagnostic tool that has applications in many areas of medicine—particularly in those areas where early, accurate diagnosis is vital such as cancer and cardiovascular disease.

The nearest NMR facility is over 100 miles from Mill Valley. With this new, life-saving technology in place at Valley General, we will be able to attract and maintain the most talented and dedicated professional staff in the region.

In order to make these plans a reality, we must reach out to the community for support. We have received a start-up grant from the State Health Department, but we need your donation to put us over the top.

Please fill out the enclosed card and return it, with your contribution, in the postage-paid envelope. Let's keep working together to keep our community well!

Thank you,

ACKNOWLEDGING DONATION

Dear Mrs. Gray:

Thank you so much for your generous donation of $100.00 to the Tri-County Library Building Fund. Every bit helps, and we are well on our way to meeting our goal for this year.

Sincerely,

Alternative Phrases:

- Enclosed is your receipt for your donation of $100.00 to the Tri-County Library Building Fund.
- Your donation of $100.00 is being put to good use as we move forward with construction of an addition to the library.
- Thank you so much for your contribution.

ANNOUNCING EVENT

Dear Dr. and Mrs. Cummings:

It's Gala time again! This year's City Hospital Gala will be held Saturday, September 12, aboard the Valejo, the glamorous and totally remodeled sailing ship dating from the 1800s.

This year the donation for the Gala is $100.00 per person. In addition to the usual gourmet meal and dancing 'til dawn, we'll have a comedy show featuring the award-winning comedy troupe, Showstoppers.

Please make your check payable to "City Hospital Gala."

Thank you for your continued support.

Sincerely,

Alternative Phrases:

- This year we'll celebrate the City Hospital Gala aboard the Valejo on Saturday, September 12.
- Join us for this year's Gala to benefit City Hospital. On September 12 we'll board the Valejo, the glamorous . . .
- The donation has been set at $100.00 per person.
- We're looking forward to seeing you there.

REQUEST TO SERVE ON BOARD

1.

Dear Ms. Reed:

We'd like to ask you to join the advisory board of the Ashville Red Cross. Your name is well known in the community, and you have a reputation for level-headed judgment.

Will you give me a call so that we can discuss the possibility of your participation?

Sincerely,

Alternative Phrases:

- We need to expand our advisory board, and we think you'd make an excellent candidate.
- Your expertise in administration, your reputation for level-headed judgment, and your influence in the community are exactly what we're looking for.
- I will give you a call shortly to get your reaction.

2.

Dear Ms. Kristen:

Larry Howard has suggested you as a possible board member for the Richardson Bay Association. Our purpose is simple: to coordinate the community efforts of artists and craftspeople along the waterfront in the preservation of the bay. Your association with Art Zone makes you an ideal candidate for our board.

Enclosed is more information about our organization. I'll give you a call next week to discuss this with you.

Sincerely,

Alternative Phrases:

- Your name has been proposed as a board member for the Richardson Bay Association by Larry Howard.
- By working with both artists and craftspeople to preserve the bay, we feel we can truly make a difference.
- I've enclosed a brochure and several flyers that will give you a feel for our organization.
- I'd like to have lunch with you next week and will give you a call to set up an appointment.

ENCLOSURE OF DONATION RECORDS

Dear Ms. Barros:

Enclosed is a record of your 19-- donations to our organization. We want to thank you for your support. You've truly made a difference.

Sincerely,

Alternative Phrases:

- The enclosed is a receipt of your 19-- donations which you may use when preparing your tax return.
- Thank you so much for your generous support. Enclosed is a record of your . . .
- You are truly valued and appreciated.

INVITATION TO MEET THE PRESIDENT

Dear Ms. Radford:

Please accept our invitation to a reception for Joelle Nelson, President of Huntington College. As you know, Dr. Nelson is not only an alumna of the college but has made significant contributions to higher education throughout our state.

The reception will be held Tuesday, September 8, from 2:00 to 4:00 P.M. at Crawford Hall.

We look forward to seeing you there.

Sincerely,

Alternative Phrases:

- We are having a reception for Dr. Joelle Nelson, Huntington College president, and we'd like to invite you to join us.
- The group will be small, so you'll have a chance to get to know this well-known educator who has made such a valuable contribution to our college.

REQUEST TO HEAD A COMMITTEE

Dear Anne:

Mike Roberts, Chair of our Fundraising Committee, is resigning, and he has suggested that you take his place. As you know, this committee is vital to our efforts to preserve historic sites throughout the county. It's also the most difficult committee we have, requiring dedication and the ability to work with people who feel very strongly about the issues. I agree with Mike that you would do an excellent job.

Will you consider the position? Please give me a call.

Sincerely,

Alternative Phrases:

- We are losing Mike Roberts, Chair of our Implementation Committee, and he has suggested you take his place.

- Because of its importance, this committee requires dedication and the ability . . .
- Your commitment and your skills make you an excellent candidate.
- I'll contact you later in the week to discuss this in more detail.

VOLUNTEER OPPORTUNITIES

1.

Dear Wally,

We need help! As the election approaches, we need people who can give us an hour or more to help with the following:

addressing flyers
walking flyers
driving
answering the telephone
making telephone calls

If you've got a minute—or longer—give me a call, or better yet, just show up at headquarters.

Thanks so much for your support.

Alternative Phrases:

- Can you give us an hour with one of the following:
- The election is almost here and, as a result, the campaign is speeding up. We need help with the following:
- You may call and schedule a time or just stop by when you're free.

2.

Dear Ms. Pender:

Thank you so much for your interest in volunteering at Bay General. The enclosed brochure describes our volunteer opportunities. As you can see, they range from office work to dealing with patients. Some require special training, as detailed in the brochure; others require no special skills. All, however, do require an application and an interview. The application is enclosed, along with a postage paid envelope.

If you have any questions at all, please give me a call.

Very truly yours,

REFUSING MEMBERSHIP IN AN ORGANIZATION

Dear Ms. Wallace:

Thank you for your invitation to join the Guild. I'm flattered and wish I had time to join and participate fully.

However, I've just signed a contract that will take me out of town a great deal over the next two years. As a result, I'm cutting back on many of my local activities and am unwilling to take on more.

Thank you again for your offer.

Sincerely,

Alternative Phrases:

- I was flattered to receive an invitation to join the Guild.
- I only wish I had the time to devote to the organization.
- I recently accepted a contract that, for the time being, forces me to cut back on many of my activities, and I cannot see my way clear to take on more.

APPLYING FOR MEMBERSHIP

Dear Sir/Madam:

Enclosed is our application for membership and our check for $25.00. Since the application form has limited space, I'd like to give you a better picture of the kind of services our firm provides.

Although this appears to be a new business, it is the result of forming a partnership and acquiring a franchise. David Westwood has been making sails in Sausalito for over ten years as Westwood Sails. Even though the name of the business has changed to U.K. Sailmakers, David will continue to offer his usual fine service. So in a sense, it's not a new business at all.

Sincerely,

Alternative Phrases:

- Since there's no room on the application form, I'd like to give you a better picture of what we're doing.
- As you can see, we have a real track record making sails in this area.

Chapter 11

INTER-OFFICE MEMOS

MEMOS CONCERNING PROCEDURES

About Long Distance Telephone Logs
About Copier Use
Keeping Track of Ad Results
Announcing Changing Hours
About Parking Spaces
About Keys

MEMOS CONCERNING SPECIAL ANNOUNCEMENTS

Notice of Mandatory Staff Meeting
Explaining New Procedures for Purchasing Office Supplies
Announcing a Promotion
Requesting Budget Information
Announcing a Holiday
Clarifying a Three-Day Weekend
Announcing an Upcoming Sale
Announcing an Upcoming Ad Campaign
Celebrating the Results of an Ad Campaign
Announcing a Sales Contest
Congratulating the Winners of a Sales Contest
Invitation to Staff Party
Car Pool Survey
Sample Style Letter

Although interoffice memos resemble letters in some ways, they are often, but not always, more informal. But, as with letters, let the content determine the tone. For example, a memo that details the legal ins and outs of a new benefit package will probably be more formal than an announcement that the parking lot will be striped over the weekend.

Interoffice memos can be used as substitutes for letters or even for verbal communications when a record is needed.

Like letters, they provide a written record, and like letters, they must be carefully thought out before they are written if they are to be an effective form of communication.

You, or your office, may choose to use a preprinted memo form, which can be handy if you're generating a single memo to a large number of people and you want to simply photocopy the number needed. Similarly, you can also set up a memo form on your computer and simply fill in the blanks as needed.

Keep in mind that while memos are simple and easy to generate, it is possible to overdo them. If your company is sending interoffice memos to all employees several times a week, employees will begin to take them less seriously. So, you may want to help management combine some of the memos, find ways to send memos only to those who truly need to receive the information, or even to propose an additional form of communication. As with all correspondence, balance is the key.

SECRETARY'S TIPS ON WRITING INTEROFFICE MEMOS

1. *Be sure you understand the purpose of the memo.* Interoffice memos are usually created to provide information to some or all employees. With this in mind, it's easy to understand why

you must be clear on the purpose of the memo. If you don't understand the information to be conveyed, it's certain your memo will be confusing. Ask yourself just what it is you want the memo to accomplish.

2. *Get all the information you need before composing the memo.* Since providing information is the purpose of a memo, be sure you have all the information you need before composing it. Your knowledge of the situation will help keep the memo clear, even if you don't address every single detail.
3. *Determine the tone of the memo.* Even though memos are more informal than letters, they can have some variance in tone. For example, a memo announcing a company picnic should sound different when read than one announcing a plan for keeping track of long distance calls.

   The "author" of the memo is also important in setting the proper tone. While your name will be proper for many memos, some will require a signature bearing more authority.
4. *The first paragraph should contain the most important information.* Memos are even easier to ignore than letters, so make sure it's easy for the recipient to get the gist of the information quickly.
5. *Make it clear what response, if any, is expected from the reader.* Many memos require no direct response from the recipient; others, like changes in parking arrangements, require an indirect response. Still others will actually ask the reader to communicate back to you or another person directly. Be sure to make it clear exactly what sort of a response is expected.
6. *Be concise and complete.* Good memos are only as long as they need to be in order to convey the proper information. Like letters, as a general rule, memos should run no longer than one page—and they are often much shorter. However, it's better to have a multiple page memo if that's what's necessary to get the job done than a short one that requires a follow-up message.

MEMOS CONCERNING PROCEDURES

ABOUT LONG DISTANCE TELEPHONE LOGS

TO: All
FROM: Martha Cooper, Secretary to Mr. Kellor
RE: Long-Distance Telephone Logs

Please remember to fill out your long-distance telephone logs each time you place a long distance call. Note the date, time, number called, person called, and the purpose of the call.

Carole or Joan in the print room can get you blank log books when you need them.

Alternative Phrases:

- You must fill out your long-distance . . .
- The long-distance log must be filled out each time you place a long-distance telephone call.

ABOUT COPIER USE

TO: All
FROM: Print Room
RE: Copier Use

As of this date we will require a "Copy Use" form to be filled out before we'll make ten or more copies. The form is self-explanatory and will be available at the Print Room window. If you'd like a supply of the forms to keep at your desk, just ask.

Alternative Phrases:

- Beginning on May 10, a "Copy Use" form must be filled out before ten or more copies can be made.

- You may request a supply of these forms for your desk at the Print Room.

KEEPING TRACK OF AD RESULTS

TO: Sales People
FROM: Stu Reid, Sales Manager
RE: Tracking Ad Results

Starting next Monday, we will be running the same ad in both the *Independent Journal* and the *Coastal Post.* We want to know which paper generates the most activity. This test campaign will last two weeks.

Attached is an ad tally form. Simply make a tally mark each time you determine which paper brought the customer in or got the customer to call.

I'll collect the forms at the sales meeting and let you know the results following the campaign.

Thanks

Alternative Phrases:

- Next Monday we will begin running the same advertisement in both . . .
- Please turn in your completed tally forms to my secretary at the end of the week.

ANNOUNCING CHANGING HOURS

TO: All
FROM: Mr. Perkins
RE: Summer Hours

Longer daylight hours mean we need to expand our hours to take advantage of customers shopping later than usual. As of May 15, we will stay open until 6:00 P.M. to take advantage of daylight savings time. Attached is a schedule showing how the extra hour will be covered.

If you have any questions, please get in touch with me.

Alternative Phrases:

- Expanded hours will begin on May 15. We will stay open until 6:00 P.M. to give our customers an additional hour of shopping time.
- Please let me know at once if this schedule change causes a problem.

ABOUT PARKING SPACES

TO: All
FROM: The Office of the President
RE: Assigned Parking Spaces

As you're probably aware, each of the parking spaces has now been given a number. Every employee will have his or her own parking space. Your parking space number is ____. Please be sure you park in only your space starting tomorrow.

We have also marked six spaces for visitors. Please direct those who are meeting you at the office to park in the visitors' parking space.

Alternative Phrases:

- You've probably noticed that each parking space has been given a number.
- Six spaces have been set aside and marked for visitors.

ABOUT KEYS

TO: Managers
FROM: Betty Oswald
RE: Keys

We have made arrangements for the front, back, and side doors to be re-keyed over the weekend. On Friday, please turn your current key in to me so that you can receive your new key.

Thanks

Alternative Phrases:

- The front, back, and side doors will be re-keyed this weekend.
- Our insurance requires that we install stronger locks on all our outside doors. This job will be done over the weekend.

MEMOS CONCERNING SPECIAL ANNOUNCEMENTS

NOTICE OF MANDATORY STAFF MEETING

TO: All
FROM: John Gray
RE: Mandatory Staff Meeting

On Tuesday, December 3, we will have our annual mandatory staff meeting at 10:00 A.M. We expect the meeting to last an hour; the agenda is attached. If you have anything else you think should be addressed, please let me know no later than November 28.

Alternative Phrases:

- The annual mandatory staff meeting has been set for . . .
- The meeting is scheduled to last one hour, and the tentative agenda is attached. I will consider additional agenda items up to . . .

EXPLAINING NEW PROCEDURES FOR PURCHASING OFFICE SUPPLIES

TO: Secretaries
FROM: Helen Johnson, Office Manager
RE: Purchase of Office Supplies

We have worked out a way to buy our standard supplies in bulk, giving us a substantial savings. The following items will be kept in the Print Room:

File folders
Paper clips
Ball point pens
Felt tip pens
Steno pads
Legal pads
Phone log books
Report covers
Correcting fluid

Gail Roberts and her staff will fill your requests; just let them know what you need.

For items not on this list, please follow the usual procedure.

ANNOUNCING A PROMOTION

TO: All
FROM: President's Office
RE: Joe Garcia's Promotion

It's with great pleasure that we announce that Joe Garcia has been promoted from his position as assistant comptroller to comptroller.

Joe brings great talent and skill to his new office, plus five years of valuable experience with our firm.

Congratulations, Joe.

Alternative Phrase:

- We are pleased to announce that . . .

REQUESTING BUDGET INFORMATION

TO: Dept. Heads
FROM: Joe Garcia
RE: Reminder—Budget Information Is Due Soon

Your estimated budgets are due next Wednesday, March 1. If you're having any problems or have questions, please let me or my staff know how we can help.

Alternative Phrases:

- Estimated budgets are due (appropriate day and date) from each department head.
- If you need assistance, please contact (appropriate person.)

ANNOUNCING A HOLIDAY

TO: All
FROM: Andrew Kay
RE: Bonus Holiday

Congratulations! We exceeded our sales goals for the last quarter, and, as promised, every employee will receive a paid bonus holiday. We will close for this holiday on July 17.

Enjoy yourself—you've earned it.

Alternative Phrases:

- July 17 will be the paid holiday promised as a result of exceeding our sales goals for the last quarter.
- Congratulations, team, on a job well done.

CLARIFYING A THREE-DAY WEEKEND

TO: All
FROM: Michael Rex
RE: Fourth of July Weekend

The Fourth of July falls on Saturday this year, which means we'll take our day off on Friday, July 3.

ANNOUNCING AN UPCOMING SALE

TO: All
FROM: Jack Hunter
RE: Upcoming Sale

Our annual inventory sale will be held from October 19–21. The attached computer sheets give you the prices that need to be changed for that event. We suggest you prepare the tags now so that they can be placed on the merchandise the day before the sale.

Alternative Phrases:

- Inventory will take place on the evening of October 21. Our annual pre-inventory sale will occur on October 19–21.
- Please prepare as many tags as possible now so that we can place them on the merchandise the day before the sale.

ANNOUNCING AN UPCOMING AD CAMPAIGN

TO: All
FROM: Bruce Lansky, Sales Manager
RE: Upcoming Ad Campaign

We've scheduled a media blitz for the week of September 7. Display ads will appear in the *Long Beach Telegram* and drive-time radio spots will be heard on KFI.

We expect this will increase the volume of business, both on the floor and on the telephone. To make it easier to handle, we've attached copies of all the ads so that you can be sure you know what we've said.

Alternative Phrases:

- An intensive advertising campaign will begin on September 7 and end on September 13.
- Attached are copies of the ads. Please familiarize yourself with the products and prices.

CELEBRATING THE RESULTS OF AN AD CAMPAIGN

TO: All
FROM: Bruce Lansky, Sales Manager
RE: Ad Campaign Results

Congratulations! The results of last week's ad blitz were tremendous, and so were you. We exceeded our expectations, and each of you rose to the challenge. Keep up the good work.

Alternative Phrases:

- Last month's advertising campaign was a success.
- We met or exceeded our goal in every department.
- Thank you for your contribution.

ANNOUNCING A SALES CONTEST

TO: Sales Staff
FROM: Helen Conroy
RE: Sales Contest

We're ready to go with our March sales contest. Here's how it will work. Gross dollar volume will be tallied at the end of the month. The top three sales people will receive a bonus. Number one will receive $150.00; number two, $100, and number three, $75.00. The prizes will be awarded at the April 15 sales meeting.

Good luck!

Alternative Phrases:

- The March sales contest will work like this:
- The awards dinner will take place . . .

CONGRATULATING THE WINNERS OF A SALES CONTEST

TO: All
FROM: Helen Conroy
RE: Contest Winners

The results of our March sales contest are in. Congratulations to Martha Johnson, first place, Peter Kelly, second place, and Jim Cocheran, third place. A job well done!

Alternative Phrases:

- Here are the winners of the March sales contest:
- Congratulations!

INVITATION TO STAFF PARTY

TO: All
FROM: Dave Wilhite
RE: Staff Picnic

Saturday, June 19, we'll have our annual staff picnic at Dumphy Park. Bring your spouse, your kids, and a pot-luck dish for five. Beverages, paperware, and cutlery will be provided.

We'll have games for the kids, games for the adults, and wind the day up with a campfire sing.

Looking forward to seeing you there.

Alternative Phrases:

- The annual staff picnic will be held Saturday, June 19, at Dumphy Park.
- Main dishes are potluck. Please bring something wonderful that will serve five.
- There will be games for both kids and adults.

CAR POOL SURVEY

TO: All
FROM: Kate Guenther
RE: Car Pool Survey

We'd like to lend our support to helping set up car pools. A preliminary look leads us to believe that enough of our employees live close to logical routes to make this worthwhile.

To get started, we're attaching a survey. Please fill it out and return it to me by next Friday, October 2.

Our plan is to set up a database that will allow us to help you locate car pooling possibilities. We expect to have the information available in about three weeks.

Questions, comments, and suggestions are welcome.

Alternative Phrases:

- The personnel department is ready to help set up car pools for interested employees.
- Please fill out the attached survey form and return it to me by . . .
- Look for more information in about a month.

SAMPLE STYLE LETTER

March 1, 1988

Ms. Susan McKinney
Engineering Secretary
E & L Engineering
3708 Concordia Blvd.
Desplatt, Georgia

Dear Ms. McKinney,

This letter is a sample of the changes we're making in our style as a result of our new logo and stationery design.

As you can see, we're using a block style. That is, there are no indents along the left margin in the address, text, or close.

Not only does this style work well visually, but it is simpler to use on both typewriters and computers.

You may want to keep this sample on hand.

Very truly yours,

Pamela Pender
Office Manager

Alternative Phrases:

- Please look this letter over carefully. It demonstrates the changes we're making . . .
- Note that there are no indentations along the left margin.
- You'll find this style actually saves time, and looks good as well.

Chapter 12

WRITING BUSINESS LETTERS AND MEMOS THAT WORK

ADDING POWER AND IMPACT TO YOUR WRITING

Powerful writing is clear writing. And clear writing is usually short, concise, and to the point. If you doubt this, think about clichés and sayings like "The pen is mightier than the sword," or "one picture is worth a thousand words," or even, "are we having fun yet?" In each case, the point is made quickly and with a minimum number of words.

Of course, there are times when you need more than a few words to express your meaning exactly. The Declaration of Independence is a good example. But notice, even though it is fairly lengthy, at least in comparison to the sayings above, it expresses complicated ideas in a succinct manner.

Be specific. For instance, if you write about *computer equipment,* you may be talking about anything from a monitor to a printer, including all the cables in between. Instead, say exactly what you mean, like the *disk drive* or the *keyboard.* If you're not sure what you mean, find out before you write the letter.

Avoid abstract words. Compare *the situation is apt to be confusing because there are no specific directions for filling out the forms* with *lack of instructions makes filling out the forms confusing.* Not only do you save nine words, but the reader will quickly understand what you're trying to say.

Here are some additional examples:

In terms of computer prices, market forces have driven the cost down, making it possible for many people to purchase systems for home use.	Lower prices mean many people can afford computers for the home.
They receive reports on a weekly basis.	They receive weekly reports.

On the issue of a wage increase, the board decided to defer the decision until the next meeting.	The board deferred action on a wage increase until the next meeting.
The addition of another secretary was considered as a solution to the problem of delayed delivery.	Adding another secretary was considered as a way of speeding up delivery.
Programming skills are considered a valuable learning experience.	Much can be learned from programming.

Another means of achieving powerful writing is by using short words. If you're tempted by multisyllabic words, think again. Short words pack more punch, and your reader is more apt to understand what you're saying. Compare:

initial	*first*
simultaneously	*at the same time*
nondescript	*dull*
fortitude	*strength*
fallacious	*in error*
sagacious	*wise*
affluent	*rich*

The words in the second column pack power; they are specific; each says exactly what you mean.

So, for powerful writing: Keep it short and keep it simple.

ACHIEVING A BALANCED WRITING STYLE

Some people, when faced with a blank piece of paper (or an empty word processing screen) tend to use language that's awkward and stilted. It's almost as if they forget how they normally speak when it's time to put words onto paper.

If you find yourself falling into this trap, stop and think of how you would convey your message to a friend. As a general rule, if you write it the way you say it, your letters will be well received.

There are business letters that need to be formal but there are not many of these in today's world. A warm, friendly, relaxed style is much more likely to get the results you want than a formal, fussy letter.

But be careful not to become too relaxed. And pay attention to the kind of business letters you're writing. Letters concerning money probably require more formality than those of congratulations.

The style of your firm will also influence the tone of your letters. For example, financial institutions tend to be more formal than many real estate firms. A large law firm is likely to have a different style than a small one.

As you glance through the letters in this book, and compare them with how you talk to your friends, you'll find just the balance you need.

GETTING STARTED

Most of your letters will probably be routine, and you'll have no trouble with them. However, as a secretary, you'll often be faced with difficult letters and find yourself puzzled about how to start them. If you're having trouble beginning a letter, consider the following:

1. *Are you clear on the purpose of the letter?* If you're clear about the purpose of the letter, try writing out the purpose on a piece of scratch paper, in ten words or less. Here are a few examples:

   <u>The purpose of this letter is to:</u>

   Get payment due us (appropriate date).
   Explain why our payment will be late.
   Offer condolences for the death of (person and relationship).
   Refusing to make a donation to (charity).

   Then, begin your letter with a filled-out version of your purpose.

Of course, you may discover that you aren't as clear on the purpose of the letter as you thought. Changes are, once you do understand exactly what you're trying to accomplish, you'll find it easy to find the appropriate beginning.

2. *Sample beginnings to get you started.* Here is a selection of beginnings that will help you get started:

   Mr. Stan Smith suggested I contact you about (subject).
   Thank you for your order, however (purpose or subject).
   We were so sorry to hear about the loss of (person and relationship).
   We are pleased to announce (subject).
   Thank you so much for (subject).

3. *Begin to write!* It may sound too simple, but often, if you'll just begin to write, the beginning will come to you, particularly when you know you're only beginning a rough draft. Once you actually see your letter, you'll be able to see what, if anything, needs to be changed.

QUICK REFERENCE TIPS ON PUNCTUATION, SENTENCES, AND PARAGRAPHS

Fortunately, punctuation need not be complicated in most business letters. An understanding of the basics—periods, commas, semicolons, dashes, question marks, and quotation marks will handle most of your punctuation needs. Knowing how to break up your letter into complete sentences and purposeful paragraphs will generally complete the knowledge you need.

PUNCTUATION

The purpose of punctuation is to make text clear. By separating groups of words with punctuation marks, you avoid ambiguity, add emphasis, and help your reader understand exactly what you mean to say.

Periods and *commas* are the most common punctuation marks used in business letters. Periods, of course, mark the end of a sentence. And a sentence is a complete thought. Commas break sentences into smaller, more manageable parts. One way to think about commas is to recognize they may occur when a pause would naturally occur in speech.

Semicolons link complete clauses into one sentence. That is, each group of words on either side of the semicolon could stand alone as a complete sentence. The clauses in question should be closely related in thought.

Dashes should be used sparingly in business correspondence, if at all. They are considered informal, and it's easy to get into the habit of using them too often. A dash is best used when no other punctuation mark seems appropriate to set off an abrupt break.

Question marks do just what they say, indicate a question. Be careful with long questions. It's easy to lose track that you're asking something, and as a result end with a period instead. In fact, it's probably better to keep your questions short in most cases.

Quotation marks are used when you're actually reproducing someone's exact words on paper. Don't use quotation marks if you're paraphrasing what someone said.

SENTENCES

Sentences are groups of related words expressing an assertion, a question, a command, a wish, or an exclamation. In other words, sentences contain one or more complete thoughts. When writing letters, it's probably best to limit the length of sentences by keeping them to one or two thoughts. Long, complex sentences, although technically correct, often confuse the reader.

PARAGRAPHS

Paragraphs are usually groups of sentences addressing a single theme or thought. Create a new paragraph when the subject changes. Incidentally, there's no reason a paragraph can't consist of a single sentence, or even a single word, although convention calls for most paragraphs to contain two sentences or more.

Your paragraphs should move from one to the next in logical order. If your letter is long and complex, you may save time by organizing it in advance. One approach is to simply list the topics you want to cover, then put them in the proper order, and write a paragraph or two about each topic.

AVOIDING CLICHÉS, REDUNDANCIES, AND TEDIOUSNESS

Although writing experts agree clichés should be avoided, what constitutes a cliché is largely a matter of opinion. A style purist said, "Never use a metaphor, a simile, or a figure of speech that you are used to seeing in print." Not a bad theory, but there's really no reason to try to avoid all familiar phrases.

Probably the best approach is to trust your own ear. If a phrase sounds trite to you, it probably should be changed, providing you can change it without creating complication or confusion.

Beware of the following:

burn one's bridges	*burning issue*
calm before the storm	*chips are down*
conspicuous by its absence	*coveted award*
dramatic new improvement	*fame and fortune*
feast or famine	*hammer out an agreement*
fortune is fickle	*from A to Z*
intensive investigation	*pillar of the community*
pinpoint the cause	*shoulder to the wheel*
take the bull by the horns	*tower of strength*
true colors	*wealth of information*

Redundancies are another potential problem. They repeat themselves, re-stating the obvious. For instance, *as a general rule* rarely means more than *as a rule* or *generally*. *In order to* can usually be changed to a simple *to*.

A crisis is by definition serious, eliminating the need for *a serious crisis*. Or how about *active consideration*? Is there any other kind of *consideration*?

Reason why is redundant—state the *reason* without the *why*, as in the *reason* I suggest this is . . . , not the *reason why* I suggest this is . . .

Even if you run out of paper clips every day, get a new *supply*, rather than *resupply*.

Make your points quickly to avoid tediousness. Use active words, and eliminate pretension. Your reader wants to know what the letter is about, and he or she wants the information delivered as simply as possible. State your purpose, explain only what needs to be explained, then quit.

A GUIDE TO NONSEXIST LANGUAGE

Our language is full of sexist terms. Most of them can be avoided by first becoming aware of them, and then by being willing to take the time to look for acceptable alternatives.

Although it's tempting to use the generic *he* or *men* when writing about men and women, it's unnecessary. Almost all terms using the male generic can be rewritten, like this:

businessmen	*business people*
chairman	*the chair*
man-made	*hand made* or *artificial*
newsman	*journalist*
salesman	*salesperson*
sportsmanship	*fair play*
workmanlike (job)	*job well done*

Often pronouns can be eliminated entirely. Instead of *A salesman may be able to increase his income with this strategy*. you could write *Sales income may be increased with this strategy*. The phrase, *a lawyer and his client* can become *between lawyer and client*.

There is good argument for using *they* as a singular pronoun. Casey Miller and Kate Swift make a case for this usage in *The Hand-*

book of Nonsexist Writing for Writers, Editors & Speakers, Harper & Row Publishers, Inc. 1980. Miller and Swift point out that language is ever changing, and that the singular *they* solves many sexist language problems and is becoming more accepted by many.

Using well-known authors, the writers make their point. For example, according to Miller and Swift, Walt Whitman wrote, ". . . Everyone shall delight us, and we them." "It's enough to drive anyone out of their senses," is credited to George Bernard Shaw. If you decide to take this approach, you're in good company.

It's also best to avoid diminutives like *gal,* or adding suffixes like *-ess, -ette,* and *-trix* when talking about women. In fact, *woman* or *women* is preferable to *lady(ies), girl(s)* or even *female(s).*

Beware, too, of assuming that professional titles refer to men. There are many women doctors, lawyers, pilots, judges, presidents, and so on. And none of them should be prefaced with the word *woman.* If her sex is important, it will show up in her name or in the reference.

When deciding what title to use for a woman, follow the same guidelines you'd use for a man. If the letter is formal and would require a Mr., use *Ms.;* if you'd address a man by his first name only, do so with a woman in the same situation.

Although *Dear Sir* is still recommended when you don't know to whom you're writing, a better approach might be to use the title, as in *Dear Manager Accounts Receivable,* or *Dear Business Person.* Or, you may use *Dear Sir/Madam* in formal situations. Some situations like this can be handled in memo form, avoiding the need to use *Dear Anyone* at all.

Another approach to this problem is to use a totally different opening, such as To Whom It May Concern. This is a bit stiff, but it does avoid picking a sex or using a generic *Sir.* If you have no real need to be formal, you might try the address, *Gentle People.* This phrase shows up from time to time. It's a nice assumption to make about the organization you're writing to, but it won't be acceptable in all situations.

Nonsexist writing takes more effort, but it's worth it. As you practice, it will become easier for you. When it works well, no one will notice the difference, and even if your usage is a bit awkward, it will be appreciated by many.

AVOID THESE MISTAKES IN WORD USAGE

Not too long ago, there was a great deal of fuss made when a popular brand of cigarette claimed to "taste good *like* a cigarette should." English teachers were quick to point out that "correct" grammar required the slogan to read "*as* a cigarette should." Ad people said the slogan wouldn't have worked if it had been correct, and most of the public wondered what the problem was. This is a fine example of how our language—any living language—changes.

There are, however, words and phrases that, while they may be common, are still not acceptable as good writing. Watch out for the following:

ad hoc	This Latin term actually means "toward this." But it's come to mean "temporary" as in an *ad hoc* committee. Far better to use the word "temporary" or "special."
address	It's become more popular to *address* a problem than a letter, but the latter is the correct use. Try *dealing,* or *taking up,* or *considering* a problem.
alot *alright* *anymore*	*Anymore* is now allowed, but *a lot* and *all right* must still be two words each.
conceptualize	This fifty-cent word really means to *envision,* which is a better word in most cases. Save *conceptualize* for truly grand ideas like the end of the universe.
interface	This is actually a technical term meaning to connect independent systems, like a printer to a computer. *Work together, coordination,* and *something in common* are all more human terms.

media	Plural for *medium,* as in television can be a news *medium.* So it's not *the media* ***is,*** it's *the media* ***are.*** This is one we may not win, and a fine example of language in the process of change.
relate to *supportive of*	Examples of weak language. She and John *are friends,* (you're describing the kind of relationship rather than using a general term) and John *supported* Mary.
utilize	A fancy way to simply say *use.*
viable	At one time, this word referred to living. If you mean *real, practical, sound,* and so on, use that instead.
viable alternative	It's unlikely you'd choose anything but a *real, practical* or *sound* alternative, so just use *alternative.*
with regard	This sounds pedantic, and it's unnecessary. Try *about* or *regarding.*

Then there are the words that are easy to confuse, like these:

Accept means to take or receive; *except* means to exempt or exclude.
Affect, a verb, means to have an influence; *effect,* a noun, is a result or outcome.
Alternately means done by turns; *alternatively* refers to options or choices.
Convince refers to a state of mind; *persuade* to action.
Complement enhances; *compliment* praises.
Expect means "to look ahead;" *anticipate* means to look ahead and do something.
Farther refers to distance; *further* refers to degree.
Fewer refers to numbers; *less* to quantities in mass.
Infer is to draw a conclusion; *imply* is to hint or signify.
Verbal refers to any use of language; *oral* to spoken language only.

A WORD ABOUT WORD PROCESSING

Word processing holds the promise of making the secretary's job easier. Corrections are easier, revisions are easier, repetitive tasks don't have to be typed over and over again because they can be stored on disk. There are programs that check spelling, programs that insert math into text, programs that merge text and graphics—the list goes on and on.

But in spite of its promise, word processing is not without its problems. The most obvious is the resistance some people have to technology. Computers and word processors can be intimidating, particularly in the beginning. Usually, however, once a person discovers how quickly changes can be made in text, they're willing to go through the learning process.

But there's another, more subtle problem with word processing. It's this: Because revisions are relatively simple, reaching for perfection can actually cause more work instead of less. Reports are beginning to surface that word processing can actually *decrease* production by as much as 30 percent in some cases.

Usually this reduction in production is caused by the people who order word processing rather than the ones actually using the word processing equipment. It's apparently the result of managers not understanding what actually happens in a typical word processing session. Because they perceive the apparent ease with which revisions can be made, they order revision after revision, reaching for some sort of perfection that probably doesn't exist. They don't recognize the following:

1. Although word processing equipment is forgiving, each and every time a file is used, you risk losing all or part of the information.
2. While it takes much less time to make a single revision, each revision does take time. The person asking for the revision spends time determining what to revise and how to revise it; the word processor must go into the file and make the revision; the revised document is then returned to its originator for additional checking.
3. Each time a revision is made, additional paper and electricity

> are used. Do enough revisions, and this expense can really mount up. Couple it with wear and tear on both the equipment and the operator, and the cost climbs higher still.

However, there are ways to reduce some of the extra work word processing can introduce. Proper planning can eliminate a great number of revisions. If the originator of the document is clear about its purpose from the beginning, multiple revisions are less likely. Some organizations are actually putting a limit on the number of revisions allowed for certain types of documents. This is particularly effective when multiple authors are involved.

Education of the people ordering word processing is another approach. Once managers begin to understand exactly what is involved, they begin to reduce the number of revisions they ask for.

Secretaries can help speed this understanding by being aware of what's actually happening as a result of word processing. Actual statistics can be kept, such as the average number of revisions needed to get a letter into the mail, increase in stationery orders, loss of data due to equipment failure, and so forth. Properly presented, this information can actually assist management in setting policy.

Word processing is both a blessing and a curse. Secretaries are in the best position to make it more of a solution than a problem.

SECRETARY'S CHECKLIST FOR LETTERS

- ☐ Be sure you understand the purpose of the letter.
- ☐ Get all the information you need before composing the letter.
- ☐ Determine the tone of the letter.
- ☐ The first paragraph should contain the most important information.
- ☐ Make it clear what response, if any, is expected from the reader.
- ☐ Be concise and complete.
- ☐ Write a draft and read it out aloud if your letter is complicated. Reading aloud will help you spot errors and confusing phrases.

- ☐ Be willing to rewrite.
- ☐ When you think you're finished, re-read your letter one more time.
- ☐ Double check the following:

  The recipient's name—make sure it's spelled correctly both inside and on the envelope.

  The recipient's title—make sure it's the right one.

  The recipient's address.

  The letter's spelling.

INDEX

G

H

I

J

L

M

N